Passport Please

An international adventure of diplomacy, intrigue, and wartime immigration

Second Edition

By Pete Nielsen

Copyright © 2007-2012 by Peter S. Nielsen

Passport Please – Second Edition
by Pete Nielsen

Printed in the United States of America

ISBN 978-0-615-59237-4

Scriptures quoted in the end notes are either from:

THE HOLY BIBLE, NEW INTERNATIONAL VERSION®
NIV® Copyright © 1973, 1978, 1984, 2011 by Biblica, Inc.™
Used by permission. All rights reserved worldwide.

Or from:

THE HOLY BIBLE, NEW INTERNATIONAL VERSION®.
NIV1984® Copyright © 1973, 1978, 1984 Biblica.
Used by permission of Zondervan. All rights reserved.

All rights are reserved solely by the author. The author guarantees all contents are original and do not infringe upon the legal rights of any other person or work. No part of this book may be reproduced in any form without the permission of the author. The views expressed in this book are not necessarily those of the publisher.

www.passport-please.com

Applause for the first edition of
Passport Please

Bobb Biehl, Founding Director of Focus on the Family:

"Passport Please takes an enormous number
of seemingly unrelated Biblical events
and weaves them into a highly readable adventure."

Amazon.com reviewers said:

"Remarkably accurate to the Bible"

"Some parts I laughed out loud"

"A cohesive, flowing tale"

"A big, big picture"

"It's not preachy"

To Linda:

*You are the love of my life,
and my partner
in this most amazing adventure.*

Regarding the Second Edition

Passport Please was first published in 2007. Thanks to all who read the first edition and provided helpful and encouraging feedback.

Five years later, this second edition includes a number of new story elements, which I hope you will find enjoyable, thought provoking and true to the Bible. Also, the endnotes in the back of the book have been enhanced and expanded.

As with the first edition, *Passport Please* does not try to prove that the Bible is true. It just assumes that it is.

Scholars who have spent decades studying the Bible still debate the possible meanings of certain Bible passages. As a novelist, I tell one, and only one story. After reading *Passport Please*, I encourage you to read the Bible for yourself and come to your own conclusions.

For information on discussion groups and the upcoming feature-length movie adaptation of *Passport Please,* visit www.passport-please.com.

I hope you enjoy *Passport Please – Second Edition*.

Pete

March 2012
Jupiter, Florida

Passport Please
Second Edition

Table of Contents

~~~

Introduction 1

1: Judgment Day 5

2: Trouble in the Frontier 11

3: King's Academy 57

4: Reclaiming the Earth 93

5: Transition of Power 131

6: Judgment Day 179

7: Kingdom Comes to Earth 185

Appendix 1: Kingdom Passport Checklist 191

Appendix 2: Endnotes 195

Introduction

The Bible is full of language describing the interactions between heaven and earth as if they were nations, with rulers, citizens, ambassadors, armies, borders, legal jurisdictions, and entry requirements.[a]

Passport Please is a story of how and why the Royals, the ruling family of heaven, established the kingdom immigration requirements, so there need not be any border crossing surprises at the gates of heaven.

Jesus gave some well-known immigration advice for those who wish to cross over into heaven—become like a natural-born kingdom citizen by being "born again."[1] Natural-born citizens are always welcome in their home country.

The concept of heaven and earth being neighboring countries was proposed by none other than Jesus himself, when He responded to Pilate, the Roman governor, by

---

[a] This book contains numerous endnotes showing the basis for *Passport Please*. When you see a small number in the story, the corresponding endnote is in the back of the book, starting on page 195.

saying, "I am a king." But he added, "My kingdom is not of this world."[2] The location of Jesus' kingdom has always been difficult to grasp. That is not surprising, since heaven is not of this world.

At the end of the twentieth century, scientists made stunning discoveries in the field of advanced physics, regarding how the universe is structured. While the multiple overlapping dimensions of string theory[3] are relatively new to the world of physics, the Bible appears to have taken the implications of this revolutionary theory for granted. Through the lens of twenty-first century physics, it is now easier to conceive of where the kingdom of heaven is, and how heavenly beings can move freely through time and space, and between heaven and the earth. Relax; no knowledge of science is needed to follow this story.

Passport Please is the story of a seven-thousand-year battle for the hearts and minds of the humans of earth. Each must choose for themselves to remain citizens of earth, or to become citizens of earth's closest neighbor, the kingdom of heaven.

Everyone chooses, even by doing nothing. One can postpone applying for a passport, but their flight to heaven cannot be postponed for very long. A 'non-decision' about applying for a passport could have huge implications at the border when they hear, *"Welcome to heaven! May I see your passport, please?"*

I hope this book will provoke fresh thinking about the kingdom to which most people say they hope to go.

❖

Introduction

Setting the Stage: The Players

The King is the patriarch of the kingdom of heaven, and is also known as the Royal Father. The King sets the vision and the direction for the nation, and is its undisputed ruler, the final authority of the kingdom.

The Prince is the Commander-in-Chief of the kingdom's armed forces. His highest aspiration is to pursue the vision for the kingdom, which is set by his father the King. He has, however, established a reputation for himself as a passionate builder and creator.

The Prime Minister is the head of the kingdom's Ministry of Foreign Affairs, which includes the kingdom Diplomatic Corps of ambassadors and consuls. The PM looks after citizens of the kingdom living outside the border, and as head of the Department of Immigration, he is responsible for conferring citizenship and issuing kingdom passports. Although the PM and the Prince are cousins, they are as close as brothers.

Michael and Gabriel are the ranking generals in the kingdom army. Each commands legions of troops, to provide security for the kingdom and to carry out kingdom missions.

Lucifer was a highly decorated general in the kingdom army, a peer of Michael and Gabriel. Known among his troops as a cunning warrior, Lucifer is skilled in reading the opposition, and in misleading the enemy into disasters of their own making. Talented, confident and ambitious, more than once he has found himself at odds with his commander, the Prince. As our story begins, Lucifer finds himself dealing with the consequences of this conflict ...

1: Judgment Day
Trial and Sentencing
◈

The main courtroom in the kingdom Justice Center was silent. Sitting forward in his chair behind the judicial bench, the Prince used both hands to close the massive book of evidence.

The balconies were jammed with celestial beings, straining to see and hear. The book closed with a thump of finality that echoed off the high arched ceilings.

Four heavily armed kingdom deputies surrounded Lucifer, the accused, who sat in silence. His eyes were fixed on his two former comrades in arms in the front row of the courtroom. Both Gabriel and Michael, the two ranking generals in the army of the kingdom, had been prosecution witnesses against him. Their eyes were fixed on the Prince.

"The Prince's poodles," Lucifer thought. "How did I ever see them as brothers? They command armies, but they are completely in the Prince's pocket. I don't think they have an ounce of free will between them."

Lucifer's mind drifted to a distant war on a distant battlefield when the three of them led their armies into battle, led by the Prince, devastating enemies of the kingdom to bring honor to the Prince's father, the King. "Hmph," he smirked slightly. "Honor to the King. Warriors face the fire but the King gets the honor. Now, if I were King, it would be different ..." He had let his opinion be known amongst the soldiers of the kingdom who served under him, and he had encouraged them to think of him as the King's equal.[1] Finally, Lucifer led his army into rebellion against the kingdom and lost. The charge against him was treason.[2]

"The accused shall stand!" thundered the stern-faced bailiff. One deputy on each side grabbed Lucifer's elbows and jolted him to his feet. Lucifer set his icy gaze upon the Prince.

The Prince returned his gaze. Lucifer felt it burn into the heart of his being, and he winced.

"Lucifer! General of the army of the kingdom and pre-eminent among the citizens of heaven, I have reviewed the evidence against you. You are accused of willful violation of the prime directive of the kingdom, which is: 'Total allegiance to the King.' *And* you have shown absolutely no remorse. Reliable witnesses have testified that you personally incited rebellion amongst those in your charge, encouraging them to turn against the kingdom and follow you in insurrection against the King. It is the judgment of this court that you are guilty of treason. Does the accused have anything to say to the court before I pronounce sentence?"

Lucifer looked over his shoulder to see his troops, thousands of warriors all wearing the dark capes of Lucifer's regiment in the kingdom army. They were a disciplined, lethal fighting force that had followed their general to the end. Gathered behind the invisible but impenetrable force field in the defendant's arena, they had

Trial and Sentencing

cast their fate with Lucifer. All of their eyes were fixed on him.

Lucifer's gaze returned to the Prince as he rose to his feet. He knew he was about to lose his rank and perhaps even be thrown out of the army. Lucifer was determined, however, that no matter what, *he* would have the final word.

Clearing his throat, Lucifer lifted his head and turned away from the Prince and toward the public gallery. He spoke in a loud voice, so he could be heard throughout the courtroom. "Citizens of the kingdom! You know that since the beginning, I have been a kingdom patriot.[3] The Royals themselves have commended me many times for my commitment and service to the kingdom. Now they call me a terrorist, and have accused me of treason. My crime? They call it rebellion; I call it fighting for *you,* the citizens. Watch now how the Royals reward those who put kingdom citizens first. Watch how they reward anyone who refuses to be a puppet on the string of this self-absorbed Royal family."

A murmur swept through the crowd. The tension that had grown between Lucifer and the Royals was well known, but Lucifer's statement was a provocative public slap in their faces. The bailiff hammered his staff on the floor to restore order. "Silence in the courtroom!"

"Indeed, you are no puppet," the Prince said coolly. "And as of this moment, you are no longer a general, either. As is the right of a citizen of the kingdom, you have been duly tried and found guilty of treason. You are hereby stripped of your rank and are dishonorably removed from the King's army, permanently."

Even though he had expected this humiliation, Lucifer still boiled inside. He thought, "Have they forgotten everything I have ever done for them ... and who I am?" Furious, Lucifer spun around to face the royal section of the courtroom gallery. His eyes burning, he focused intensely on the Prime Minister. "Take your damned kingdom citizenship as well!" he bellowed. "I don't want it!"

A collective gasp could be heard in the courtroom as all eyes went from Lucifer to the Prime Minister. The PM closed his eyes at what amounted to a total renunciation of the kingdom and the Royals.

After a moment of silence, the Prince, the King, and the Prime Minister exchanged glances. The King, sitting next to the Prime Minister, nodded silently. The Prime Minister looked at the Prince and said, almost inaudibly, "So be it."

"So be it!" the Prince repeated, loud enough for everyone to hear. "Lucifer, you have publicly and willfully renounced your citizenship in the kingdom of heaven. Your renunciation has been recognized by the Prime Minister. As of this moment, you are no longer a citizen of the kingdom.[4] Accordingly, you are to be deported and confined to the lower frontier."

Still burning with rage, Lucifer began to process the consequences of his sentence. In his mind, he rationalized, "At least we'll be across the border and away from these overbearing Royals. The frontier is not like heaven, that's for sure, but the old royal garden down there used to be pretty nice.[5] And, I will be in charge again, free from the stench of that Royal family.[6] Yes," Lucifer concluded, "I can deal with this."

Turning to the defendant's arena, the Prince addressed the captive army.

"Army of the kingdom under Lucifer! You were misled by the one who is now about to be exiled. He has brought you to the brink of condemnation, but not yet into it. Your leader has fallen and you shall be deported with him, but hear this! You need not be exiled forever."

"You were trained well and you have been loyal to the authority placed over you, however corrupt that authority

Trial and Sentencing

may have become. Choose your destiny while you are in exile! A final judgment awaits you."[7]

To no one's surprise, the faces of Lucifer's soldiers showed only contempt. Disciplined to the end, they drew strength from their leader's defiance of the Prince. Lucifer stood silent and proud.

"So be it," said the Prince. "Lucifer, your pride has led you into darkness. Bailiff, carry out the sentence. Escort the prisoners to the portal!" The Prince hammered his gavel, stood, and turned to exit the courtroom.

An army of heavily armed kingdom deputies moved forward to surround Lucifer and his soldiers. They moved the condemned army out of the courtroom, toward the edge of the massive Crystal Sea portal, the gateway to the lower frontier of the kingdom.[8]

The lower frontier is an expanse of undeveloped territory belonging to the kingdom, but spanning far fewer dimensions than the kingdom proper. Lucifer knew that when he and his army fell through the Crystal Sea onto the earth, in the middle of the long-neglected royal Garden of Eden, they would be bound with dimensional restraints. They could only move in the dimensions of the lower frontier, and would be kept from reentry into the kingdom by means of a very secure border.

Lucifer and his soldiers were led out of the courtroom, down a road leading to the portal. In a final act of bravado, Lucifer stopped suddenly and turned to his army. He raised his clenched fist and shouted, "Follow me to freedom from the King!" He turned toward the portal and together, the entire condemned army let out a shout, "FREEDOM!" With thousands of defiant fists shaking in the air, they ran down the steep hillside, over the edge of the cliff, and into the Crystal Sea, disappearing from the kingdom of heaven.

Lightning crashed across the sky as the portal swallowed them up, and its glassy surface closed behind them. The condemned leader and his army fell, as if tumbling down a dimensional staircase, into the lower frontier.⁹

2: Trouble in the Frontier
Establishing the Garden Colony
※

Between the marble floors and high arched ceilings of the great kingdom hall and the throne room, the atmosphere was one of eager anticipation. The tiered walkways lining the walls and crossing over the hall were filled with thousands of kingdom officials and staff bustling back and forth, attending to the business of heaven, and making last-minute preparations for the start of the Immigration Project.[1]

Light poured through the tall windows, brightly illuminating thousands of flags hanging along the walls, representing dominions and regions in every corner of the kingdom.

The great kingdom hall is the preeminent building of the kingdom and can be seen from the far reaches of heaven. Behind the king's throne, floor-to-ceiling windows looked out over Crystal Sea, through which Lucifer and his army had been deported. From this waterfront vantage point, the King had an unobstructed view through the sea and into the lower frontier. Often, he had swiveled his throne around,[2] slid the massive windows open and rested his feet on the edge of the balcony while he pondered the future of his lower frontier.[3] Today, the pondering was over and the plan was about to unfold.

The King was seated on his throne overlooking all the activity, waiting expectantly for his son.

The Prince strode confidently into the great kingdom hall, excited and prepared for the challenge ahead. It was to be an adventure that would change *everything*. He and his father had been planning the Immigration Project for a long time. Expanding the borders of the kingdom around the lower frontier had been their favorite topic of conversation since Lucifer's rebellion had been put down.

Earth, in the lower frontier, can be seen by the residents of the kingdom through the Crystal Sea portal; but ever since the rebellion, it hasn't been much to look at. It is mostly covered with water and is a dark and empty place.[4] Many kingdom residents had heard about the Immigration Project, in which the entire lower frontier was to be redeveloped and annexed into the kingdom proper. They knew that Lucifer and his army had been banished to the lower frontier long ago, so this project was certainly going to stir up some excitement.

As if skating on ice, the Prime Minister of the kingdom slid across the surface of the Crystal Sea, toward the great kingdom hall and throne room. He was squinting, looking down at the dark earth below the sea, and thinking about the kingdom expansion into the frontier and all that it would mean. It would mean a lot of new citizens immigrating into the kingdom, for one thing, and orderly immigration was the Prime Minister's bailiwick. The PM glided onto the throne room floor and greeted the King and the Prince. Together, these three Royals, the ruling family of the kingdom, were about to launch something big.

The King waved his hand for quiet in the room and said, "It's time." The noise level in the great hall dropped,

Establishing the Garden Colony

but the activity around them continued as a thousand conversations transitioned to whispers. The King motioned for the Prime Minister and the Prince to come closer. "It's time to restore the lower frontier. We'll light it up with a great cosmos and populate the earth with living beings—humans—members of our Royal family. And when we extend the kingdom borders around the earth, we'll go there and live with them."[5]

"Son, this project is under your authority. You are going to make it happen. These humans will be your people, your nation. In the end, heaven and the earth will become a united kingdom."[6] The King gripped the back of his son's neck with a fatherly squeeze, as the Prince beamed.

As a general, one of Michael's primary jobs was security and protection for the kingdom and for the Royals. Stepping forward, he hesitated a moment, not wanting to dampen the mood. Then he spoke, "You know that Lucifer will consider your colony on earth to be an invasion of his territory."

"He *knows* the lower frontier was never his to begin with," the King responded.

"Correct," The Prime Minister added, "But the facts don't matter to him. He'll claim squatter's rights, or whatever legal maneuver he can come up with to assert his authority."

"He will do anything he can to humiliate us and to derail the Immigration Project," the Prince agreed in a somber voice. "He hates us, but that is certainly no surprise."

"So be it," the King said with authority. "We are expanding the borders of the kingdom around the lower frontier, whether Lucifer likes it or not. How he responds to our presence there is for him to decide, but he will live with the consequences of whatever actions he takes."

Michael nodded slightly, satisfied that he had done his job by raising the issue, and secure in the knowledge that the Royals had taken these matters into account long ago.

The Royals stood quietly for a moment and the King broke the silence, "You know, son, preparing the earth and building our colony will be the easy part. Raising up a family of patriots who love the kingdom will be the hardest thing you have ever done."

The Prince nodded. He was ready.

The Royal Father looked at the Prince and said, "It's all yours, son."

On the earth below, Lucifer walked bitterly through the dark, barren, and soggy earth in the company of his soldiers.

"This place is nothing like it used to be, but I'd rather be in charge of this wasteland than groveling in heaven," he told his army, outwardly defiant. Lucifer was fully aware of the strength of heaven's border security, and the hopelessness of attempting a forced reentry. Confined to the dimensions below the kingdom gates, the lower frontier was their prison.

"Damn you, Prince!" he shouted at the invisible kingdom when none of his troops were looking, shaking his fist in no particular direction.

The Immigration Project was the number one priority in the kingdom, and all of heaven's resources were standing ready. Members of the kingdom Corps of Engineers assembled before the Prince, who was flanked by his generals, Michael and Gabriel.

In a clear, loud voice, the Prince shouted, "Stand ready to expand the borders of the kingdom!"

The Prince stepped into the Crystal Sea portal and disappeared under the water. He entered a dark storehouse where everything was ready and waiting. Looking down, he spoke the ignition code, setting off a series of atomic reactions. He quickly stepped back to just below the kingdom border, and watched.

The reactions grew almost instantaneously into an outpouring of matter and energy never before seen anywhere in the universe. Brilliant light, violent energy, and an unimaginable amount of solid matter tore across the emptiness and began to form a whirling cosmos. Energy from the explosion burst all the way to the top of the kingdom, more than ten dimensions up, flashing through the surface of the Crystal Sea and into the King's throne room.

On the barren earth, Lucifer and his army shielded their eyes, seeking escape from the searing light, heat, and energy. "What is going on?" he shouted, though no one could hear over the roar.

As artifacts of the cosmic explosions roared off into the near and far reaches of the lower frontier, an enormous ball of fire spun toward the earth and shined bright, steady beams of light onto the previously dark planet. The first dawn on the earth was absolutely magnificent.

The edge of the King's mouth curled upward in a smile. He nodded to Gabriel, who in turn addressed the Corps of Engineers in a loud voice, "You know your part in the plan! Now GO!"[7]

At his command, wave after wave of kingdom engineers followed the Prince down through the surface of the Crystal Sea. The portal swallowed them up as they shot through into the lower frontier.

"Let's put some space between the earth's surface and the Crystal Sea portal," the Prince shouted to his team. Looking up at his father, he added with a wink, "But not so far that the King won't be able to see it from that big throne of his."[8]

The fireball had dragged several planets, some of which in turn dragged along moons of their own. It's gravitational pull finally proved irresistible, and the earth tore loose from its moorings beneath the Crystal Sea. An open, empty sky filled the space between the water on the earth's surface and the Crystal Sea in the kingdom above.[9]

The Prince liked what he saw and looked at his father, who nodded in approval. He deployed a team of kingdom engineers onto the wet, spinning earth. The Prince tasked some of the engineers with pooling the oceans, others with shaping the continents, and carving the rivers. The Prince's detailed plans even included a global plumbing system for irrigating the land with clean, fresh water. That was critical, given the unimaginable number and variety of plants and trees that were being planted just about anywhere there was dry land.

The earth was shaping up well in all its dimensions. The Prince had several other teams of kingdom engineers at work establishing the distant planets, stars, and galaxies. To the engineers crafting the earth, it seemed like the work went on for ages. The Prince, however, confidently assured them that it all would be complete within a few days. Of course, *time* is one of the dimensions running through the lower frontier, and all the kingdom engineers knew what Einstein later discovered, "time flows at different rates, depending on whose watch you are using!"[10] They knew that the Prince was the one keeping time.

Birds, fish, wild animals, livestock—each was designed specifically for life on the three dimensions of earth. It was all coming together.

Lucifer was speechless. He watched from the shadows while the Prince refurbished the once-formless earth. "He's turning my prison into a paradise again," he thought. "Is the King extending an offer of peace and reconciliation? Has he finally realized the mistake he has made? It took a while for him to admit it, but I think the King is coming around!"

Establishing the Garden Colony

Lucifer was unaware that a survey team of kingdom engineers was busy redrawing the maps to include the earth and the higher dimensions in the lower frontier (what they called "the heavenlies") as a colony of heaven. This was the first step in formally extending the kingdom borders around the entire lower frontier. As the surveyors moved closer to the earth, Lucifer moved closer to losing his status as the freewheeling frontier warlord on this dismal swamp. He was on his way to becoming an undesirable alien in a colony of the kingdom of heaven.

The frontier was ready. The time had come for the centerpiece of the Immigration Project, the first human being.

The Prince wanted to create the first human personally, with his own hands. Later, the PM would come alongside these newest members of the Royal family, to teach them everything they needed to know.

With a nod to his father and the PM, the Prince once again stepped down through the Crystal Sea portal and entered the lower frontier.

The Prince knelt in the dirt of his newly renovated earth. He plunged his hands into the moist clay and carefully, artfully formed the first man. It was a marvelous, complex creation. Bending over, the Prince drew a breath and breathed into the man, the breath of life. Royal blood started circulating in the man and he was alive. The Prince called the man Adam.[11]

The crowd gathered around the portal in heaven was amazed. They all watched as the Prince looked upon the newest member of the Royal family, asleep in the grass. The Prince flashed a huge smile, looked up through the portal, and said to the crowd, "Man, this is good." The crowd erupted into applause.

The Royal Father nodded in agreement and added, "But not so good if he is going to be alone down there!"

The man would not be alone. He would have the Prince by his side and the Prime Minister as his teacher, but the Prince knew exactly what his father meant; Adam needed a wife.

Before Adam woke from his sleep, the Prince called Michael, Gabriel and their squad leaders to show them the first human member of the Royal family.

On the edge of the meadow, just beyond the tree line, Lucifer had been watching as the Prince created Adam. He was curious, frightened and angered all at once. He could not just stand by any longer. Taking a deep breath, Lucifer walked toward the Prince and the soldiers. As he approached, the kingdom warriors instinctively snapped their hands to the hilts of their swords. The Prince turned toward Lucifer, and with a slight move of his hand, motioned to Michael to keep their weapons sheathed.

The Prince and Lucifer had not been face to face since that day in the kingdom Justice Center when the Prince handed down his verdict, hammered the gavel, and deported Lucifer and his army from the kingdom into the lower frontier.

They stood and looked at each other. Finally, the Prince broke the silence. "So, where have you been?"

Lucifer bowed slightly. "Roaming through the earth. I must say, you have restored it far beyond its original beauty."

The Prince nodded to acknowledge the compliment. "Have you seen my greatest creation?" he asked gesturing toward the sleeping Adam. "We call him a human being. He is intelligent and creative. He will know the truth and will turn his back on evil."[12] Lucifer blinked at the inference. "And he's a full-blooded member of our Royal family."

That struck Lucifer like a hammer. He thought, "Just what I don't need on my earth—another stinking Royal!"

Knowing he had to respond, Lucifer collected himself and smoothly floated his proposition.

"Of course he'll be all those things, oh Prince," he said with a patronizing smile. "He has no choice."

Michael and Gabriel stiffened as the tension mounted. The Prince looked Lucifer in the eye and let him continue.

"Is there anything off limits for the man? Why not draw a line in the sand? You can tell him all the reasons why he absolutely must not cross it. And let's see what the human does when he is given a real choice."

Michael and Gabriel looked at each other, aghast at their former comrade's brashness. The Prince did not blink.

"You said he is intelligent." Lucifer paused. "Intelligent enough to choose between your truth and mine ...?"

The Prince looked down, shook his head and responded, "Lucifer, you don't even know what truth is. Lies are your native language."[13] He sighed deeply. "Very well, the man will choose. You may speak to him, but you may not lay a hand on him or any other human."

"Understood," Lucifer responded, almost unable to contain his excitement. "And if he chooses to turn his back on you, will you hand him over to me?

The Prince did not answer right away. Glancing up, he saw his father watching. Their eyes met for a moment. The Prince looked down at Adam and said slowly, "If the man chooses to turn his back on us and follow you, I will hand him, and all that he has, over to you."

Michael and Gabriel could hardly believe what they were hearing.

"This man and the entire human family are free to make their own choices," the Prince spoke in a strong, steady voice. "But understand this, Lucifer. Every detail of my father's plan will come to pass. I guarantee it."[14]

Lucifer bowed with feigned respect while stepping backwards, withdrawing from the meeting. He turned quickly and bolted into the trees.

The Prince watched Lucifer disappear into the forest, then he looked at the sleeping human. "And so it begins, Adam. The enemies of the Royals are now the enemies of man."[15]

Adam and the Prince became friends. They enjoyed exploring together, walking through the earth, marveling at the newly created creatures and enjoying the abundant food. The earth was full of plant life, including an outstanding garden of fruit trees—pears, nectarines, passion fruit, kiwi, bananas, cherries, apples, lemons—to name a few. "Delicious and nutritious!" the Prince said to Adam, as he sank his teeth into one of them, juice dripping down his chin. "It's not that I don't enjoy the other trees, it's just that if a tree doesn't produce good fruit, it isn't nearly as useful. You can always tell a good tree by its fruit."[16]

It was a great experience for both of them, wilderness camping and hiking amongst the wildlife in the virgin forest. They would sit around a fire in the evening and just talk. The Prince was eager for a close relationship with Adam. Their conversations lasted late into the night.

"So there is even more to the universe than all of this?" Adam asked, poking his stick at a smoldering log while gesturing with his head toward the star-filled sky.

"Oh yes," responded the Prince. "There are many dimensions here in the lower frontier, each separate and distinct, but all occupying the same physical space. So far, you have only seen a few of them."

Adam pondered his place in the universe, not really knowing where to begin. "How can all the dimensions occupy the same space?" he asked.

"Remember the flocks of birds we saw today?"

Establishing the Garden Colony

Adam nodded. The Prince continued, "Well, a bird can move in the up-down dimension, no matter where it is in the east-west or north-south dimensions. All three of those dimensions, length, width and height, overlap each other, and occupy the same space. Time is like that as well. No matter where the bird flies, the dimension of time overlaps its physical position."

They sat silently for a while as Adam thought about living in multiple dimensions simultaneously. He poked the log again and it broke, exposing a glowing core.

Adam asked, looking directly into the Prince's eyes, "So you can sit here with me, then get up and move into a dimension where I can't follow you, or even *see* you?" He half expected the Prince to get up and disappear.

"I can, and I do, often," smiled the Prince, not moving from his seat on the log.[17] Adam nodded and looked back at the log's glowing center and jabbed it, sending up a shower of sparks into the shower of stars above.

"Here, take a look at this." The Prince pulled out a map of the kingdom and the lower frontier. "It's not to scale, but I think you'll get the picture ...."

(see map on next page)

Running his finger over the map, the Prince explained, "As a human, Adam, you can move freely in the three physical dimensions of the lower frontier—length and width and height. Time runs through all of them, and there are a few invisible dimensions which you can't see. We call those "the heavenlies." There is still a lot to explore here in the garden, but all these dimensions? They're *nothing* compared to what is up here," he pointed out on the map, "in the kingdom proper."

Passport Please - Second Edition

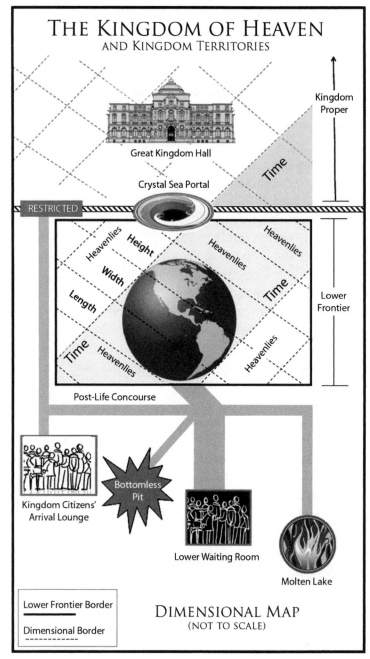

" I came from up here," the Prince said, pointing to the great kingdom hall. "Long ago my father established a barrier, actually more like a moat, on the border of the kingdom proper, separating it from the lower frontier."

Adam thought that was interesting. "He did that because...?"

That is a story for another day, my friend," smiled the Prince, deciding that the tale of Lucifer's rebellion could wait until later. "But when the kingdom proper and the lower frontier are finally united, the barrier will be removed. Then you will be able to move in *all* of the dimensions of the kingdom, like I do."[18]

"So why are we here now?" Adam asked, not fully understanding the importance of this question, or the answer he was about to hear.

The Prince lifted his eyes from the map and looked at his friend. "My father wants to expand the kingdom by growing our family. The Immigration Project is not just about moving the borders of the kingdom outward. It's about *you* being part of the Royal family."[19]

Adam looked down and smiled, not sure what to say. On the other side of their campfire, a pair of furry ring-tailed animals waddled through the firelight and disappeared into the darkness. Adam asked, "How about them?"

"No, they're not family," the Prince chuckled. "Not like you are anyway. They have bodies, and their own mind, will and emotions, but that is where the similarity between you and them ends. They are part of the kingdom, but they will never be kingdom royalty." The Prince looked off into the woods. "So," he asked, "what do you call those things?"

Adam thought for a moment. "Uh, raccoons, of course."

"Raccoons," the Prince nodded thoughtfully, "of course." They both laughed.[20]

After a while, Adam looked back at the map and tried to grasp what the Prince had told him. "You said that *time* is one of the overlapping dimensions here in the lower frontier." The Prince nodded. "So I can walk back and forth in time? It feels like right now I am just being pulled along by time, at its own pace, not mine."

"You're right, Adam. Time runs through the lower frontier like a river. You *are* being pulled along by it now, but when the Immigration Project reaches its conclusion, humans who are citizens of the kingdom will be able to walk freely in every dimension, including time. Just like I do," replied the Prince. "That's what we call eternal life. Time never runs out, any more than east or west runs out."

"When do we get to that part of your Immigration Project?" Adam asked, ready to be an eleven-dimensional man.[21]

The Prince laughed, "You just got here, man! What's your hurry?"

Adam tried to keep from smiling, but did anyway.

"My father and I have high expectations for you, Adam," the Prince explained. "You will need to learn about kingdom law and justice, and about the authority and responsibilities you will have as a kingdom citizen, and as a Royal. The Prime Minister and I will teach you all these things."

Adam was out of questions for the night. He already had a lot to process. It had been a long day and he was ready to get some sleep. The heat of the day had turned comfortably cool. The embers of the fire flickered in the gentle breezes, and a choir of crickets provided background music.

"I'm sure it will all make sense in the morning," Adam said as he lay back on the grass and looked straight up at the stars. "G'night Prince."

"I'm sure," smiled the Prince. "Good night, Adam."

That night as Adam slept, the Prince planted two special fruit trees in the middle of the garden. He called the first one the "Tree of Life" and the other he called "the Tree of Knowledge of Good and Evil."[22]

Eating fruit from the Tree of Life would nourish Adam's body, enabling him to walk in all the dimensions of the lower frontier, including the heavenlies, and of course, the dimension of time.

Though he couldn't do it yet, Adam, like all humans, had a body designed to walk back and forth in time, as easily as one might walk back and forth through a field of grass. Eating from the Tree of Life would allow Adam to enjoy a life where time never runs out. Without nourishment from the Tree of Life however, he would simply be pulled along by time until his human body clock wound down and eventually stopped.

The Prince planted "the Tree of Knowledge of Good and Evil," to draw his line in the sand. The next day, he looked Adam in the eye and told him clearly, "Do *not* eat from this tree. If you do, you will *die*."[23]

For Adam, the new world was full of mysteries and the Prince's command not to eat from that tree was only one of them. He didn't give the tree a second thought. He was more interested in his next safari with the Prince.

That night, the King's words echoed in the Prince's heart. "It is not good for the man to remain alone on the earth." It was time for the Prince to let his human friend begin the Royal family line on earth.

Once again, the Prince personally created a human being with his own hands. He wanted a real "oneness" between the man and his wife, so this time he didn't use the dirt of the earth, but rather, he surgically removed a bone and tissue sample from Adam. Beginning with those, the Prince constructed a woman. She had dark, beautiful eyes, delicate hands, long thick hair and a shape that made Adam's heart pound. She was stunning.

The Prince was pleased. She was a perfect mate for his friend Adam.

Adam was, of course, delighted. He called her Eve. The Prince joined them together by presiding over the first marriage ceremony, right there in the garden. Now they were one, not only physically, but legally as well. The Prince pulled Adam aside for a bit of advice, "Adam, you need to love this woman more than you love your own life."[24]

As a wedding gift, the Prince gave Adam and his bride authority over the earth and everything on it—all the animals, birds, fish, plants, and trees on the whole planet.[25] "Everything on the earth now belongs to you, and you belong to our family," the Prince told these first Royal colonists in the lower frontier.

Adam took his bride on long walks through the meadows of the garden, showing her the places where he and the Prince had explored. She particularly enjoyed being introduced by Adam to the sheep, the horses, and other animals which roamed the garden, showing no fear of the humans.

"They're all ours?" she asked as she stroked the wooly head of a lamb that had come up and nuzzled her.

"All ours," smiled her husband.

Opposition and Legal Settlement
ఇ‌ఇ

Unbeknownst to Adam and Eve, they were not alone in the garden. Besides the animals and fish that filled the forests and waters, they were sharing the lower frontier with Lucifer and his army of followers.

Lucifer had been watching them, along with two of his lieutenants. "The Prince thinks these creatures made from dirt are going to rule my earth," he said, breaking into an evil smile. "The Prince banished us from the kingdom for violating his prime directive. Now, isn't it ironic—these humans are about to go down the same way."

His lieutenants nodded, not sure what their leader was thinking, but confident in his leadership, nonetheless.

"The Prince is so proud of his so-called kingdom justice," Lucifer continued. "Watch how I get these stupid humans to spit in his face and follow me. If the Prince wants to maintain justice, he will have no choice but to keep them out of heaven, just like he kicked us out of the kingdom. If he doesn't, he has only two options; he can either go home and leave the lower frontier to me, or he can declare amnesty and let us *all* back into the kingdom. Anything else and he will be exposed as the hypocrite he truly is!"

The former general moved on his objective—the woman. She had heard the command about the tree, not from the Prince, but second hand from her husband. Lucifer entered the garden when neither the Prince nor the man was in sight. He found Eve and entered into a friendly conversation with her. When he asked her about the Tree of Knowledge of Good and Evil, Eve responded by reciting the Prince's command, just as Adam had told her, "We will die if we eat from that tree—or even if we touch it!"

"Eve, I think you've misunderstood what the Prince meant when he spoke with your husband," Lucifer smiled, intrigued by her embellishment regarding "touching" the tree.[1] "The Prince isn't always as clear as he ought to be. You won't literally *die*. He was saying that when you eat from that tree, your *ignorance* will die, and you'll be as wise as he is. That's why it is called the Tree of Knowledge."[2]

He had her attention. She wanted to be seen as wise.

"The Prince knows that you will be like him when you eat that fruit. You really could be like him. You *should* be like him. Trust me." He extended his hand with the fruit.

Eve looked at the fruit. "The Prince will appreciate us more when we are as wise as he is," she rationalized.

"Of course he will. You seem to be getting smarter already," Lucifer nodded, smiling.

She took a bite. The juice gushed out as her teeth broke through the skin of the fruit into the sweet soft flesh, which melted in her mouth.

Moments later, Adam arrived at the center of the garden and saw what Eve was doing. "These are really good, Adam," she said with juice dripping from her lips, "I've got to believe that this is really okay. You know, getting knowledge and all. Here, have one."[3]

Lucifer held his breath in anticipation.

Opposition and Legal Settlement

Watching from the edge of the Crystal Sea above, thousands of collective breaths were being held as one.

Adam's mind was racing. There was no mistaking what the Prince had told him. The consequences had been made terribly clear. If the Prince had spoken the truth, Eve had just crossed the line and she was as good as dead already! Adam realized that meant he'd never be with his wife again! He began to panic.

He thought, "What if the Prince's warning was really just a figure of speech? No! Why wouldn't he mean just what he said? Is the Prince a liar? Of course not!" Adam knew the Prince. He had lived and walked and talked with the Prince. The Prince was no deceiver. "If I eat what she is offering," he thought, "we'll both die. If I don't eat it, my wife will die alone—and the Prince just told me that I need to love her more than I love my own life."

As if standing on the edge of a rushing river watching a loved one being swept away to their death, Adam came face-to-face with the hardest decision of his short life. Overcome with love for his wife, but knowing full well that he had no hope to offer her, Adam made his choice. Taking the fruit from the hand of his beautiful yet condemned bride, he took a bite, knowing it was all wrong.[4]

He had effectively jumped into the raging river and grabbed hold of his wife, all the while thinking, "What have we done?" The safety of shore receded swiftly.

Lucifer smiled, thinking, "Tough times require tough choices. Welcome to my world, humans."

As promised by the name of the tree, both Adam and Eve began to gain knowledge immediately—knowledge of fear, fear of the Prince, fear of the Prince finding out what they had just done.[5] They had chosen to follow this stranger in the garden instead of the one who had given them life. They were now both as good as dead, according to the

Prince. Adam grabbed his wife's hand and they both ran into the bushes.

Adam explained their dilemma to Eve. She responded, "What kind of crazy rule is that anyway? Knowledge will make us more like him. What's so bad about being like the great builder of the kingdom? Hey, we can build things as well!"

Eve reached for a nearby fig tree and pulled down a few giant leaves. With the help of some thin vines, she created a coat for her husband and one for herself. "Now, there you go," she said, adjusting his new outfit. "That's much better than running around naked. You'll see. The Prince should be quite impressed. He'll see our ability to improve ourselves and he will respect us for it. Trust me."

Adam saw some logic in his wife's statement, and he *was* impressed with the clothing she had created. Suddenly he remembered what the Prince had said, and his heart skipped a beat. Adam knew the Prince was a man of his word.

At sunset, they heard the Prince call out, "Adam! Hey Adam! Where are you?" Adam and Eve hid for a while, then finally stepped out from the bushes, both suddenly embarrassed at the clothing that they had fashioned for themselves. The Prince stood before them, taking in the moment. He shook his head slightly at the sight of their ridiculous wardrobe.

"OK Adam, what happened?" the Prince said. "Did you disobey my command and eat fruit from that tree?"

"This wife you gave me offered me the fruit. She had eaten some already, so I had no choice but to eat it with her."

"Sounds like you had a choice and you made it," said the Prince. He turned to Eve, "And your story?"

"He lied to me," she said, pointing at Lucifer, "and I believed him."

Opposition and Legal Settlement

"Let me rephrase that for you," the Prince said, "you trusted him instead of me." Eve looked down at the ground in silence.

The Prince turned to Lucifer. They both knew the terms of the deal.

Lucifer wanted to crack a defiant smile, but couldn't bring himself to do it. In spite of his apparent victory, Lucifer was still very intimidated by the Prince.

The Prince looked at Lucifer with eyes of steel. "You think with one lie you can drag them down into the dust with you? Take a good look at this woman you tricked; one of her descendants is going to crush your head.[6] Lucifer, you have no *idea* who these humans really are."

Looking again at Adam, the Prince said, "I told you not to eat fruit from that tree. I know exactly what you did and why you did it. Regardless of your reasons, your actions have consequences. The laws of the kingdom apply here in the frontier. Otherwise, there would be no order in the territory. Here's what you need to understand about kingdom law: "Willful disobedience to kingdom authority is *treason,* and treason is punishable by *death.*"[7]

"If the judge finds anyone guilty of treason, they will have to pay with their own life. That is, unless their debt, their sentence of death, is paid for by someone else."

"Treason?" Adam stuttered. "All we did was eat some fruit. That's treason?"

"You're right," replied the Prince. "All you did was eat some fruit. You did the *only* thing I told you *not* to do on the *whole* planet. Sorry Adam, kingdom law does not recognize big or little acts of treason, only treason."

"We get the death penalty for eating fruit?" Adam asked, incredulous.

"You didn't listen to what I said," the Prince responded. "Yes, all treason merits the death penalty in the kingdom, but under kingdom law, someone else *may* take your punishment for you, *if* they are qualified. To be your substitute under kingdom law, they must meet three qualifications. First, they must be innocent under kingdom law, not under condemnation themselves. Second, they must *willingly* accept your punishment, the death penalty. And third, they must be a member of your household, not a random stranger."

Adam and Eve were trying hard to follow what the Prince was saying, but kingdom law was all new to them.

"OK," Adam said slowly. "Who will do that for me?"

"Don't worry," responded the Prince. "I will provide the One you need."

Lucifer was fully aware of this provision in kingdom law, but he was not sure how it applied to this situation. His mind began to race ...who could qualify as their substitute? Under kingdom law, it had to be from the human's family.

"Who could be in their family and be *the One*?" Lucifer wondered. Then it hit him, "Crusher! The Prince promised that the woman's descendant would crush my head! The Royals want to crush me, and free the humans from death row in one shot!"

Lucifer reflected on that for a moment and concluded to himself, "I don't have a plan to deal with this yet, but understanding the problem is half the challenge."

"You establish a death penalty for treason, but you show traitors how to escape?" Adam asked the Prince, trying to understand the logic behind kingdom justice.

"Exactly. The only ones who will have to die are the ones who refuse to accept the King's pardon. Trust me," said the Prince. "All you have to do is admit your guilt and when it's offered, accept the pardon. But until we start issuing kingdom pardons," he explained, "you need to do your part."

"Which is ...?"

Opposition and Legal Settlement

"Like I said, admit your guilt, and then offer the King a substitute from what I have given you—a substitute that will take the punishment for your crimes."

Adam was really trying to follow, but ...

"Here," said the Prince, "Let me show you."

The Prince turned his head slightly and listened. Through the bushes, they all heard the rustling sound of the lambs ripping up grass and munching on it. "Are those your lambs?" the Prince asked Adam, already knowing the answer. Adam nodded, feeling sure that he was not going to like what was coming next.

The Prince turned and strode into the bushes. A few minutes later he returned with blood on his hands, carrying two robes made from sheepskins.[8]

"Now," said the Prince, "take off those fig leaf creations of yours. They can't cover what you have done. Cover yourselves with these." He held out the robes to the man and the woman.

Adam and Eve stood in silence, aghast at what they were witnessing.

"Awful, isn't it?" said the Prince.

"But what *you* did is awful ..." Eve blurted. Adam put his arm around her, hoping she would hold back, but she couldn't. "Those beautiful sheep—they didn't do anything wrong. They're dead! Because of *us*?"

"You are right, Eve, on all counts," the Prince responded. "These sheep were innocent, willing substitutes that took your punishment for you. If you accept that their lives satisfied the death penalty, which hung over your head, then you will be free. If you don't, then their deaths will have been for nothing and *you* will face the death penalty."

"We recognize that offering up the lifeblood of these animals is the closest you can get to satisfying kingdom law until I provide the One, the perfect substitute, who can take your punishment. These animals resemble the One in each of the three requirements, but they don't *quite* qualify.

First, the animals *are* innocent, not under condemnation, *but* they lack the human sense of right and wrong.

Second, the animals *are* willing, as beasts of burden, to carry even this burden for you, *but* they don't comprehend the significance of their sacrifice.

Third, the animals *are* from your household, since I gave all the animals to you, *but* they are only animals, not humans from your family."

"So they don't *exactly* qualify as a substitute, but it's the best you've got until I provide the One to take your punishment for all time," said the Prince, "Do you understand?"[9]

Eve wasn't really listening to the Prince. She blurted, "But they're dead! How could you be so cruel?"

The Prince responded like a father addressing a child who cannot possibly understand the magnitude of a problem or its solution. He asked, "Eve, do you know what happens to animals when they die?"[10]

"No," Eve responded.

"Well, *I* do," responded the Prince. "I made them, and I know *exactly* what happens when they die, but the explanation involves things that your human mind simply cannot comprehend while you live on the earth." He paused. "Look around at *everything* I've made and *everything* I've given you. Can you trust me on this?"

"I suppose," she said quietly, realizing more than ever how much she didn't know.

The Prime Minister, seeing what was unfolding in his colony, stepped down through the Crystal Sea with a large envelope under his arm. He walked through the garden and whispered in the Prince's ear, "It's time to get them out of the garden and away from the Tree of Life."[11]

Opposition and Legal Settlement

The Prince nodded.

Looking at Adam and Eve, the Prince said, "I told you that you would eventually walk freely in all dimensions of the lower frontier, including time. I planted the Tree of Life so when you ate its fruit, you could live forever. Well, you have chosen a different path."

"Today," the Prince said somberly, "you must leave the garden and live on the earth. You will walk freely in the three physical dimensions of the earth, but not in the dimension of time. Until the judgment you will be a prisoner of time. It will sweep you along and carry you to the kingdom courtroom where you will face the judge."[12]

Not knowing exactly what that meant, the man and his wife pulled their lambskin coats a little more tightly, as the evening had begun to turn noticeably cooler.

Lucifer was taking it all in, trying to put the pieces together in his mind.

The Prime Minister tapped Lucifer on the shoulder and signaled for him to step to the edge of the garden. The PM spoke softly to him, showing Lucifer the envelope, and discussing it.

The Prince continued to speak with Adam and Eve, "You were the first residents of the kingdom's colony on earth. I appointed you as rulers over the earth, under my authority." There was a note of sadness in his voice. "But you turned your back on me and followed a new leader. By disobeying the *only* directive I ever gave you, you aligned yourselves with …" he paused as his eyes moved to Lucifer, " with that snake."

They looked over at the Prime Minister and Lucifer, who were concluding their discussion.

"By your choice," he hesitated, "this earth I gave to you is now under the legal authority of the warlord Lucifer, and you are both now citizens of *his* earth. But remember," the Prince continued, "a Royal never takes back a promise.

Trust me, everything ultimately still belongs to me, including you. Even though you have chosen to follow Lucifer, in the end I will get back what is mine."[13]

Adam and Eve waited in stunned silence, as their entire world turned inside out.

Lucifer and the Prime Minister finished their discussion. The PM walked back to speak privately with the Prince.

Quivering with excitement, Lucifer could hardly contain himself. He looked for a moment at the humans and smirked, then bolted from the garden. As he retreated, Lucifer was ecstatic, thinking, "These Royal humans will be locked in the three physical dimensions of earth and we will be all over them in all the heavenlies! They'll never even see us coming. Now that's what I call authority! Back in the saddle again!"[14]

"Is everything written down?" the Prince asked the Prime Minister. He was referring to the terms of the transaction handing over authority of the earth from Adam to Lucifer.

"Absolutely. Signed and sealed. No doubt you will need it later," the Prime Minister responded confidently.[15] "We will hold up our end, but Lucifer will certainly try to find a loophole."

The Prince shook his head, "It was the *only* kingdom directive I *ever* gave them, and such a small one!"

"It's time," said the PM. "Send them out of the Garden, away from the Tree of Life."

The Prince looked at Adam and his wife. "Go now, down to the earth. Live there and work until your bodies wear out and die. In time, you'll face the judge in the kingdom."

"Our bodies will die? What exactly does *that* mean?" asked the man, still unclear about most of what had just transpired.

Opposition and Legal Settlement

"When you go down the path leading out of the garden, you'll leave all this behind," the Prince explained. "And you'll live out your lives in the three dimensions of earth. You will be swept along by time until the mainspring of your body clock winds down and stops. Then your body will return to the dirt you came from.[16] Your body will die, but *you* won't. After a while, you will both face kingdom justice —on the charge of treason."

This was almost too much for Adam and Eve to bear. In what seemed like a moment, they went from an adventurous, exciting life with the Prince in the garden, to an uncertain future in a strange place, under the authority of the Prince's enemy.

"Take heart," the Prince said. "You are still my family. Remember what I told you about the One who can clear your kingdom record? Until he comes, remember what I showed you. You need to regularly offer back some of the animals I gave you, so you will be in good graces with the judge when you stand before him."

They stood in silence, looking at the Prince, not really wanting to leave.

Like a parent disciplining a child, yet suffering with them, the Prince finally said, "Leave the garden, *now*."

Adam and Eve walked down the path, away from the garden. They glanced back as a mist closed in behind them. Their minds raced with uncertainty and fear. They had no concept of what lay ahead. At the bottom of the path, they walked out into a dusty field. Looking back, they saw a kingdom guard brandishing a sword at the entrance of the path, but that too was fading away.[17] Soon, they couldn't even see the entrance to the garden path, just the dust and dirt in the three dimensions of earth.

The Prince and the Prime Minister returned to the kingdom proper.

The polished wooden table dominated the glass-enclosed conference room just off the throne room in the great kingdom hall. The King presided over the meeting from the head of the table, flanked by his son the Prince, and the Prime Minister. Generals Michael and Gabriel sat opposite each other, further down the table.

"Permission to speak freely?" General Michael asked.

"Absolutely," nodded the King.

"What you are doing is amazing," Michael began. "These humans will receive an incredible gift, the opportunity to have their record wiped clean, and to become citizens of the kingdom again. But it is clear that they don't appreciate or even understand what you are doing for them. To them, Prince, you look—forgive me—like an ogre."

"Some might view it that way," replied the Prince. "But having them understand my plan completely, or even for them to *like* me is not an immediate goal of the Immigration Project. In time, that can come, but for now, I'll settle for respect, even if they think I'm being too harsh. Eventually they will realize that there is nothing I wouldn't do for them—*nothing*."

"There is no other way to bring them back into the kingdom," said the King. "If we don't treat kingdom violations with the deadly seriousness they deserve, the humans will never take them seriously either."

"I know," said the Prince, gazing thoughtfully out the window, down at the earth through the Crystal Sea. "I know."

Adam and Eve settled in their new domain. It was nothing like the garden; that was for sure. They couldn't put their finger on it exactly, but everything just seemed so flat and gray after the richness and vibrant colors of the garden, which was quickly becoming a distant memory.

Opposition and Legal Settlement

They worked hard for their food, but the Prince had personally instructed them on the art of plowing, planting and threshing their grain so they could now enjoy bread.[18] They began to raise a family, and in time, their family farm prospered.

Lucifer was quite pleased at the way things had developed. From here on out, everyone born on his earth was, by birth, a citizen of earth and subject to him. "The Prince isn't the only one who can be a nation builder," he said to himself. "These humans may be the Prince's family by blood, but from now on, they'll be citizens of *my* earth, by birth."

The Prince regularly left the kingdom, crossed the border to visit with Adam and Eve and their little family, *his* family. He was anxious to strengthen the relationship which had been strained in the garden.

Adam and Eve appreciated the Prince's visits and they had come to recognize that despite the hardships of farm life, the prosperity they enjoyed was a direct result of the gifts which the Prince had given them: the land, water from the sky, the flocks of animals. Their friendship grew, as together they established Adam and Eve's family on earth.

Adam, however, was still occasionally haunted by the words of the Prince in the garden, "You are guilty of treason and someone has to pay ..." Adam knew that he and his wife had foolishly crossed the line in the garden; there was no arguing with that. He knew that they still crossed the line on earth, and they could usually trace it back to their own selfish behavior. At least the Prince had shown them the way to getting right with kingdom law, offering back from what the Prince had freely given them.

Adam and Eve had two sons, Cain and Abel. Both young men understood from their parents about offering back the best of what the Prince had provided, as a substitute for when they crossed the line. They knew that the kingdom's prime directive was a line that they selfishly wandered across on a regular basis. Cain and Abel were glad to offer back to the Prince the best of what they had, to keep their kingdom records clean.

Cain, being a farmer, offered to the Prince the best of his farm, fresh-baked breads made from the grain he grew in his field. Abel, a shepherd, slaughtered the best lamb from his flock for the Prince. Both brothers offered the Prince the absolute best they had in their household. They were determined to do better than their parents did in the garden.

The Prince accepted Abel's sheep with appreciation. "Kingdom law is no threat to you Abel!" the Prince said approvingly.

Cain was absolutely speechless when the Prince told him that his offer of bread was inappropriate. He couldn't believe that the Prince was so ungracious and ungrateful.

"I worked hard to grow the grain," Cain protested. "I kept the birds away from it, harvested it, ground it, kneaded it, and baked it!" In his anger, he raised his voice at the Prince, "All my brother did was watch those stupid animals grow, and then he killed them! Don't I get even a little respect for my effort?"

"Son," the Prince said, "let me teach you something really basic. If you don't understand this, you won't understand the kingdom at all. No human on earth can live up to what is expected of a Royal. The consequence for treason is death, and that's why you need a qualified substitute to take your punishment, so you can live."[19]

Cain's eyes were down. He shook his head and mumbled, "Uh huh, I *know*. I brought you a substitute—a *good* one."

"Hey, look at me." The Prince put his hand on Cain's shoulder and gave him a fatherly look, straight in the eye. "Your bread doesn't qualify. It is the work of *your* hands,

Opposition and Legal Settlement

your planning, *your* time, *your* efforts. Understand this, Cain; your life-work doesn't cut it as an acceptable substitute, but what will is the *lifeblood* of an innocent, willing substitute in your household. That is something only *I* can provide, and it will clear your record. You *can't* get right with the kingdom by your *own* efforts."

"That's it, Cain. Your bread smells great, but you need to get yourself an animal to offer back. Trade for it if you have to. Once you own it, kill it and bring it to me. That will be an acceptable substitute to take your death sentence, and kingdom justice will be satisfied. Clear your record or your record will eventually kill you. This isn't just a good idea, Cain, it's the law."

The Prince stood quietly, allowing what he said to sink into the young man's consciousness. A long minute passed silently.

"What-*ever*," said Cain as he turned his back to the Prince and walked away, feeling totally rejected. "That Prince has no idea how hard I worked to provide that bread for him," he thought. "My bread *ought* to be good enough for him. He has no respect for me or what I can do. If he does, he certainly doesn't know how to show it."

Later that day, he found his brother Abel in the field, watching what Cain had called "his stupid animals." Cain's frustration turned to anger. Lucifer whispered, "Just do it," and Cain's anger turned to murder. Abel bled to death in his field as the sheep watched silently.

Lucifer and several of his soldiers sat and watched the entire scene from one dimension up, out of human sight. "I don't think this is exactly what the Royals had in mind when they fixed this place up and started their little family on earth," he cackled, "but I like the way this is shaping up."

Abel was a natural-born citizen of the earth, and Lucifer was eager to take custody of the first human to

41

depart the planet. "Bring him on down," he said to his assistants.

Lucifer was referring to bringing Abel's soul into the lower waiting room, which had been prepared for human citizens of earth whose earthly bodies have died.[20] They wait here for the judgment, which the Prince had spoken about. Since the lower waiting room is a facility for citizens of earth, Lucifer has management and administrative authority over it. The ambiance of the room reflects the warmth that Lucifer feels toward his human subjects; it is not comfortable at all. The lower waiting room is basic at best. There are thousands of rows of wooden benches, and there aren't many lights. The high, sealed windows let in a glow from the outside, but it never seems very bright, and the slowly turning ceiling fans only stir the dusty air.

Lucifer's soldiers approached Abel's body and suddenly stopped dead in their tracks. A tall, intimidating warrior of the kingdom had appeared out of a dimension above them all and was lifting Abel's soul out of his body.

"Hey! Leave him alone! He's ours!" Lucifer's troops shouted.

The kingdom warrior straightened up and looked down at the two, who were now wishing they hadn't used that tone of voice. "This one is ours," he replied. "He is an honorary citizen of the kingdom by his Royal bloodline. Besides, the Prime Minister has authorized me to bring him to the kingdom citizens' arrival lounge." He waved a paper at them.[21]

They didn't care to get close enough to read it.

"Don't worry. I'm sure you'll find some humans to take care of soon enough," the warrior said as he went back to his task.

He lifted Abel's soul to the kingdom citizens' arrival lounge.

Opposition and Legal Settlement

Both the kingdom citizens' arrival lounge and the lower waiting room are located on the edge of the lower frontier, on the fringes of the dimension of time. While time flows through the lower frontier and the earth like a river, in the arrivals lounge and the waiting room, the flow of time is barely a trickle. While waiting for the judgment in either place, a thousand years on earth seem to pass in a day, if one is not paying attention.[22]

If the lower waiting room has the ambience of a bus station at dusk, the kingdom citizens' arrival lounge is more like a replica of the great kingdom hall, with light streaming in through the tall windows, plenty of comfortable seats, snacks and drinks, all managed by an attentive staff from the kingdom Department of Immigration. This lounge is the post-earth counterpart to the lower waiting room, established for humans who on earth had clearly demonstrated a pro-kingdom lifestyle, and had consequently received honorary kingdom citizenship.

Abel had faithfully offered up qualified substitutes, and the Prince and Prime Minister had conferred honorary kingdom citizenship upon him. When the One who was promised by the Prince had done his work, Abel would be eligible for full kingdom citizenship. Until then, honorary citizens of the kingdom wait in timeless comfort.

"Welcome Mr. Abel," the lounge attendant greeted his first guest, "May I get you a drink?"

On earth, shortly after the murder, the Prince confronted Cain in the field. "Don't think you can just walk away from this!" he shouted, "Listen to me![23] Do you have any idea whose blood you spilled today? That was Royal family blood! My family blood!"

"I showed you how to come out from under the condemnation of kingdom justice, but your pride wouldn't let you take what I offered you." The Prince made no attempt to hide his displeasure. "Cain, you are *done* with being a farmer. In fact, you're done with this land. Get out of here and wander through the earth for the rest of your life. You don't want to be subject to kingdom justice? Fine. It's your choice. You can try living life outside the law, but understand this—an outlaw finds no protection under kingdom law! Unless you first get right under the law, you'll find no sympathy from the kingdom judge."[24]

"But if I'm outside the law, anyone who finds me can murder me!" Cain pleaded. "You're sending me out to be killed!"

"Oh, I see. So *now* you think murder is a *bad* thing," the Prince said with more than a hint of sarcasm.[25] Reflecting for a moment on the fear he saw in Cain's eyes, the Prince said, "Don't worry, I will see to it that when people see you, they will know that I am protecting you. Anyone who kills you will bring a double helping of kingdom justice down on their own heads."[26] The Prince reluctantly sent the son of his friend Adam out into the wilderness. "Get moving, Cain."

The Prince saw Lucifer and his soldiers watching, but he didn't care. In fact, the Prince wanted Lucifer to hear his warning about staying away from Cain.

Locals Attack - Kingdom Response
❦

As the years went by, Adam and Eve had other sons and daughters.[1] The population of humans on the earth grew. The men were strong and many lived well past one hundred years, and the women were very easy on the eyes.

The humans spread across the face of the earth, as if they owned it. The soldiers who had been ejected from the kingdom to earth with Lucifer were closely watching the Prince's family. The soldiers enjoyed watching the women. They *really* liked to watch the women.

A few of his troops approached Lucifer requesting that he would let them take up permanent residence in the lower three dimensions of earth. They wanted to introduce themselves to a few of these women, start up a friendly conversation, and see what developed.

Up until this point, Lucifer had wanted to keep his soldiers physically separated from the Prince's family, lest some in his army might be tempted to turn back to the kingdom. But he thought about what the Prince had said, "One of her descendants is going to crush your head."

"So, one of the descendants of the Royal family on earth is going to crush my head," Lucifer mused. "The Prince seems to be putting a lot of faith in the downstream potential of his Royal family here on earth. I think perhaps a little tinkering with the bloodline is just what this family needs. Who knows what could develop?"

"These humans are natural-born citizens of my earth," he mused. "Hmmm. If they are part of *my* bloodline, they will be citizens of my earth by their *bloodline* as well as by birth. So if the Crusher then comes from their household, there will be no question that he's *my* boy, not the Prince's."

Satisfied with his own logic, Lucifer turned to his troops and said with a grin, "Why not? Go for it!" Those of his soldiers who moved down to the earth had no trouble finding human women who eagerly embraced them and had children with them. With fathers who had been higher-dimensional beings, it came as no surprise that these offspring grew to be physically huge. They were known far and wide for their superhuman strength—and their cruelty to other humans. People called them "the Nephilim."[2]

Lucifer enjoyed watching this unfold. He was pleased that the Prince's Royal bloodline was now competing with his own.

"There's more than one way to deal with this Royal family," he thought. To Lucifer, the prospect of becoming a Royal in-law seemed just too hilarious.

Lucifer was riding high. The people of earth grew less interested in the kingdom, and more interested in getting ahead—bigger farms, more gold, more cattle—just *more*.

Thanks to the antics of Lucifer's soldiers, the humans were losing their Royal bloodline, removing them from any claim to being part of the Prince's kingdom family on earth.

The lower waiting room was filling up with a steady stream of deceased citizens of earth. Most of these guests had committed themselves to living successful lives, had minimal bloodline ties to the Royal family, and showed no interest in the kingdom.

Locals Attack - Kingdom Response

"We are back in business!" Lucifer joked with his lieutenants. "The Prince may have grabbed Abel and a few others, but don't worry. There will always be some kingdom loyalist fanatics we can't get our hands on, but everybody else? They are mine! Hah!"

Lucifer's humor was appreciated neither by the Prince nor his father. It became clear that humans were on a path to self-destruction and with Lucifer's encouragement, they made a mockery of kingdom law. The King said sadly, "I am fed up enough to wipe the slate clean on earth and start over. Mankind is nothing but murder, violence, selfishness, and grief!" He sighed, "Let's let the floodwaters reclaim the earth."[3]

"Wait," pleaded the Prince, reaching out for his father's arm. "There's a man who is still like us down there. His name is Noah. He is loyal to the kingdom and is a pure, full-blooded Royal. None of his ancestral bloodline has been polluted by the enemy."[4]

"You are absolutely right about how despicable the humans have acted, Father," the Prince continued. "When left to themselves, they have always chosen a path of self-destruction. Let's do as you say, Father. I will wipe the slate clean on earth and begin again, but let me start again with this man Noah and his family. Then, when we restart the earth, I will stay close to them and I'll form them into the nation of heaven on earth. I will lead them and protect them and, together with the Prime Minister, will send them to the King's Academy, to teach them the ways of the kingdom."

The King's Academy was the school that the Prime Minister had designed for the Prince's nation, to teach them what it means to be part of the Royal family. The academy had no buildings. The world was its campus. Here they would learn hands-on lessons in loyalty, justice, law, and government. It was all part of Adam and Eve's choice to gain knowledge of good and evil. It was also part of the Royal's plan to educate and raise their family on earth.

The King and Prime Minister acknowledged that the Prince's plan was the right thing to do, but they were all fully aware that the bad seed sown by Lucifer was going to be trouble for generations to come.

"OK son," the King said, "time to save the human race from destruction ..."

" And the animal kingdom as well," chimed the PM.

"Of course," said the Prince with a grin. Excited about the fresh start, the Prince went to the earth and spoke directly to Noah, providing all the information and materials Noah needed to build the ship that would save his family from extinction.

When Noah and his family had completed preparations and loaded the animals, as the Prince had directed, Noah sent his wife up the ramp into the boat. He called to his three sons, "Boys! Time to go! Drop what you are doing and get your wives onboard."

Two of Noah's sons had married local girls, but his middle son, Ham, had chosen a beautiful, tall wife from a neighboring region. No one in Noah's family knew much about her background, but they loved her as if they had known her all their lives. That was good, because it was going to be close quarters for the next year.

Once all eight were on board, the Prince slammed the door shut behind them and said to the assembled team from the kingdom Corps of Engineers, "Pour it on."

At the Prince's command, a team of kingdom engineers turned the wheels of the floodgates above and below the earth, covering the planet with water. Everything and everyone on the earth who breathed air, died. Everyone that is, except the one man with the pure Royal blood in his veins, and his family.

Locals Attack - Kingdom Response

As the tainted human bloodline on earth was being washed clean, the lower waiting room was dealing with a surge of human citizens from earth, but it was nowhere near capacity.

Already, several of the lights in the lower waiting room had burned out and none of the staff there seemed interested in replacing the bulbs. The brightest light came from the flickering screens with a video feed from the kingdom citizens' arrival lounge. Watching the comfortable, casual setting of the arrivals lounge, without being able to go there, only served to mute the atmosphere in this already drab place.

Newcomers would always ask, "How do we get to the arrivals lounge?"

If they could coax an answer from a waiting room staffer, it was always the same. "You can't get there from here."[5]

"It's a new day, Noah," the Prince said as they stood looking over the now dry earth. It had taken almost fourteen months for the floodwaters to rise, recede, and finally yield to dry land. It had been a long and frightening voyage, surrounded by death.

When they landed, Noah knew the first thing he needed to do was to recommit himself and his family to the kingdom on the newly cleaned up earth and claim it for the kingdom. He did it by offering back to the Prince some of the animals he had brought along, just for this purpose.

The Prince was impressed, "You really do get it, Noah. Right from the start, you are keeping your kingdom record clean with the blood of these animals from your household. That blood will make you honorary citizens of the kingdom. As your family spreads out across the earth, feel free to eat the meat of animals, but not their blood. Don't eat it, don't drink it, and don't take it for granted.

Remember to use the blood only to get right with the kingdom."

Noah and his family unloaded the ship and got back to the business of tending the land and their flocks. Lucifer's attempt at hijacking the Royal bloodline had been thwarted, or so it seemed.

Noah enjoyed planting and tending his vineyard and became expert at making his own wines. One day, after Noah had sampled way too much of his own vintage, Ham found his dad, naked and unconscious on the floor of his tent.

"This is just too funny," Ham thought. He ran out and told his brothers—who didn't think it was funny at all. When Noah later awoke, he was furious with Ham and cursed him for having gossiped to his brothers about Noah's indiscretion. Ham packed up his wife and children and settled far away in what was later called Palestine.[6]

Over the years, Ham's family grew, but not just in numbers. Like his wife, the children of Ham grew tall and strong—some of them were actually giants. This came as a surprise to Ham, but not to his wife, who told him she had brothers and cousins, before the flood, who were over seven feet tall.[7]

Drawing the Battle Lines
ৎ◈৶

After some reflection, Lucifer decided he was impressed with the Prince's gutsy move, killing virtually everyone and everything on the planet. Recalling the Prince's burning gaze in the kingdom Justice Center so long ago, he thought, "This Prince is no softy. He is a certified fanatic." Lucifer was coming to the sobering realization that the Prince would never allow his conviction to be overturned. Groping for ideas, but coming up short, he thought, "I *need* to find a legal loophole."

Lucifer shook his head and let his anger keep him from sinking into depressive thoughts. "Dammit, this flood was an illegal act by the kingdom!" he shouted, hoping the Prince would hear. "This is *my* earth! We have a *deal!* You have no business meddling in the local affairs of *my* earth!"

Composing himself, Lucifer was determined to find an opportunity to strike back at the kingdom. He thought, "I can *do* this. I will take these humans down somehow and turn this entire lower frontier into a killing field. Either the humans will do the killing or the Prince will do it again himself. Either way, no humans will get to be part of his kingdom!"

Over time, the human population got big and got busy. If they even had time to think about it, the reasons for "that flood" long ago were totally irrelevant to their busy lives. The earth's pioneers had a can-do attitude, relying on themselves to make things happen. In the city of Babel, for example, some of the more ambitious people launched a project to construct a massive skyscraper, just so they would be known throughout the world as the ones who designed and built such a colossal tower.[1]

The Prince shook his head in dismay. "I was hoping they'd want to be known as the royalty of the kingdom on earth. It seems that for these people, 'What we *do*,' has replaced 'Who we *are*.'"

Lucifer was not dismayed in the least. "This," he thought, "will be the foundation of my plan! These humans are no different from the two in the garden. They just want to be recognized for their own wisdom, their accomplishments, and their ambitions."

Lucifer gathered his lieutenants around him and began to rehearse his marketing plan. He explained how they would win and hold onto the hearts and minds of the humans.

"They all want to be successful. I can help them get what they want. After all, I respect their wisdom and accomplishments, as a great leader should. I, for example, would never have turned Cain away like the Prince did. *My* earth is a "meritocracy." Here, humans earn respect from me and from other humans by what they do—for their beauty, their accomplishments, and their wisdom—not through some barbarous, bloody ritual."

Lucifer knew that his plan was a winner, and his lieutenants agreed. He aimed to keep the attention and the allegiance of most, if not all, of the Prince's humans.

Not surprisingly, the Prince had an altogether different view regarding his "meddling in local affairs" as Lucifer

Drawing the Battle Lines

called it. He knew that the kingdom was the ultimate owner of the lower frontier, and Lucifer's authority would not last forever.

Under kingdom law, when anything belonging to the Royal family is lost, whether through misfortune or mismanagement, it is not lost forever. The Prince knew that, under the terms of their deal with Lucifer, the earth would eventually revert back to the kingdom. At any time the earth could be bought back by a member of the Royal household on earth who is qualified, willing, and able to pay the price.[2]

"I am really glad you wrote it all down," the Prince said to the PM. "Lucifer knows full well he is obligated to accommodate our right to buy back the earth. You can never trust a snake with just a handshake."

"We both know he is going to try to scam us," the PM said. "He thinks he can void everything by letting his soldiers have sexual relations with the women of your nation. Through their children, Lucifer will try to hijack the bloodline of our Royal family on earth."

The Prince nodded, "Lucifer thinks he can stop us from opening the gates of heaven. He wants to tie this whole deal up in a custody battle. He will claim that the One, the Crusher, is really from *his* household, not ours—so no one will be qualified to enforce the provisions of the mortgage."[3]

"For safekeeping, I had the mortgage sealed and stored in the kingdom archives," the PM said. "I have no doubt we will need to invoke the penalty clauses in another six thousand years or so."[4]

Lucifer was very well aware of kingdom law and the terms of his lease on the earth. He also knew he could scam just about any deal, written or not. He was the expert on "managing situations."

"Without having their kingdom records permanently wiped clean," he thought, "the humans won't survive their judgment any better than I survived mine. If I can disqualify the Prince's substitute, even those so called honorary citizens in the arrival lounge will all be doomed." Lucifer concluded, "Then the Prince will have three choices—destroy all his precious humans, go home and leave all the humans to me, or let us *all* back into the kingdom."

Lucifer pondered the facts as he knew them, "The Prince said that Crusher would be a descendant of the woman in the garden—a human. He'll also have to be completely innocent under kingdom law, living a life of total allegiance to the King; but I've never seen a human who could keep their record totally clean—not one."

He didn't know the answer yet, but he kept thinking of how he could cut off the Crusher. Lucifer knew that he had stepped on the Prince's nerves by allowing his soldiers to intermarry with the human women. The Prince had been so upset, that he was willing to wipe out almost the entire planet to put an end to their behavior.

"I am definitely on the right track here," Lucifer mused.

It was all coming together in Lucifer's mind, and he was very excited to see a way to unravel the Prince's plan. Lucifer smiled a smug grin. Calling his lieutenants together, he explained the situation. They were in awe of their leader, of how Lucifer had seen right through the Prince's plan.

"We've got a three-pronged attack strategy here," Lucifer began. "First of all, keep an eye out for a human baby, probably a boy, who will be born into the Prince's nation. The Prince told me he will send this One specifically to crush us all. We are the legal rulers of earth and the kingdom is trying to crush us! We have got to stop this terrorist."

Drawing the Battle Lines

He continued with instructions for his officers, "You all need to listen to what the humans are saying. If anyone gets wind of this boy's arrival, do whatever it takes to kill him. I don't care if we have to wipe out a whole generation of boys, just get him!"

His staff nodded with determination, ready to defend the earth from kingdom terrorism.

"Second, every good plan has a Plan B. I trust you, but I also know what a sneak the Prince is. If somehow we miss our target and the boy slips through our net, we must make sure he has no weapons to use against us. Here's how we are going to take away his ammunition. We will continue to aggressively insert ourselves into the Royal bloodline. Then, if this boy does show up, *I* will be his daddy! We'll claim he's in *my* household, not the Prince's, and the DNA will back us up! Nobody will be able to buy back the earth and the agreement will be void. In the end, we'll see whose head gets crushed."

Once again, Lucifer authorized a number of his most trusted soldiers to aggressively pursue the women of the Royal family on earth. "And while you're at it, let them know that sex is a gift that is meant to be enjoyed *by* everybody, *with* everybody. Share the goodness!"[5]

"Third, while they are getting on with the ladies, the rest of us will be out and about, encouraging the humans to commit themselves totally to following their own dreams. These humans will be so consumed by their own busy lives, that even if little Crusher can somehow clear their kingdom record and get a pardon for them, they won't care one little bit. "They will blow off the Prince exactly the same way my man Cain did ... 'What-*ever!*'"

Lucifer knew his plan was a winner. "The Prince may think he's got a deal, but he's got *nothing!*"

3: King's Academy
National ID System

If the Prince is a builder at heart, the Prime Minister is a teacher through and through.

"At the King's Academy, we will teach your people the principles our kingdom rests upon," the Prime Minister explained to the Prince. "They'll learn by repetition, and they'll have a lot of lab work. They will get firsthand knowledge of what is good and what is evil. They will find out what works and what doesn't work in the kingdom."

"It should become very clear to them why kingdom immigration policy must be as strict as it is," said the Prince. "Why we can only let kingdom citizens in." He smiled and added, "It *is* very edgy of you, holding classes out here on the street. That's where the *real* learning always takes place."

"Absolutely!" said the PM. "That's why we've got our national ID system, designed to help keep the King's Academy students in, and the troublemakers out!"

Noah was still alive when his descendant Abram was born in present day Iraq. The Prince went to meet with

Abram in his home with a simple yet stunning message: "You have been chosen to be the founding father of the kingdom's nation on earth."

Though Abram wasn't perfect, the Prince knew he had found his man. The Prince shared his vision for the nation, "This is going to be a great nation, Abram, with more people than there are stars in the sky. Someday, everyone on the earth is going to reap the benefits of your nation's special relationship with the kingdom and with me."[1]

"But understand, it takes extreme pressure and extreme heat to make a diamond, Abram," the Prince continued. "I will send your people to the King's Academy, the most difficult of schools, but they will learn to trust me, and learn that I will *always* defend and rescue them. Your nation's enemies will be my enemies and your nation's friends will be my friends."

At the Princes direction, Abram packed up his entire household and moved to the land of Canaan, some five hundred miles to the west. He was ready and willing to start building this nation, but, "You *do* know that I am eighty-five years old," he said to the Prince, somewhat dubious about having a child, "and my wife is no youngster either. I have no idea how your plan could work."

"Just trust me," said the Prince. "I have you covered."

Lucifer was amused, thinking, "Perhaps Abram's wife Sarai can help him think through this little conundrum." He chuckled, remembering the incident in the garden, "Déjà vu!"

Sure enough, Sarai, just trying to be practical, suggested that Abram could start this nation by having a child with their lovely young au pair from Egypt. Without a moment's hesitation, Abram, man that he was, went along with his wife's suggestion. At eighty-six, he became the proud father of Ishmael.

National ID System

The Prince was understandably disappointed. "This is *not* what I had in mind for you Abram. Ishmael is a fine boy, and from him will come the mighty nations of Arabia, but his descendants will be nothing but trouble for our nation for the next four thousand years."[2] The Prince implored, "Would you just trust me when I tell you something? I really *do* have you covered, Abram."

It took more than another ten years, but the Prince finally came to Abram and said, "It's time to start that nation we talked about. But first, from now on, you will be called *Abraham* and your wife will be called *Sarah*. I don't want anyone to say *you* made a name for yourself as the father of your country. *I* am the one who will make a name for you Abraham."

The Prince continued, "By this time next year you and Sarah will have a son." Sure enough, at the grand age of 100, Abraham had a baby, a son named Isaac.[3]

"Its absolutely amazing," Abraham said to the Prince, as they both looked at young Isaac in Sarah's arms.

"Abraham," explained the Prince, "you, Sarah, and Isaac are part of a 100% pure Royal bloodline, right from the kingdom of heaven. The warlord of this earth will try everything he can to hijack our Royal bloodline. As a matter of national security, we cannot let that happen."

Abraham and Sarah were surprised that the Prince's nation had just started and they already had attracted powerful enemies.

"This is how you will keep it pure—no one in this nation of mine shall have sexual relations with people from outside of my nation.[4] This is imperative. It is the only way you can protect my Royal bloodline."

"Little Isaac is only a few days old now. When he is eight days old, I want you to cut off his foreskin, circumcising him. Do this for every son born into my new nation," the Prince explained. "And do it for all the men who are now in your household." He paused, "Yes, Abraham, even yourself."

Abraham swallowed hard and just looked at the Prince. Neither Abraham nor Sarah were clear on why cutting part of their son's manhood was so important for national security, but the Prince had their full attention.

The Prince continued, "This circumcision is a man's proof of citizenship in the kingdom's nation on earth, our national identification system."

"When any woman in my nation gets married and is about to have intimate relations with her new husband, one look at his manhood and she will immediately know if that man is part of my Royal bloodline. If he is *not* circumcised, she will know he is *not* one of us, and if that is the case, she is *not* allowed to have sexual relations with him. No excuses! She can call out to her brothers and they will deal with the intruder.[5] My Royal bloodline in this nation *must* be protected from those who would pollute it."

"So outsider *men* are the only threat to the bloodline?" Sarah asked, "What about the outsider *women*?" thinking of Hagar, her servant-girl-turned-rival.

The Prince understood. He looked up and with a nod called down a squad of kingdom security agents who cordoned off a secure perimeter around them. What the Prince had to say to Abraham was not for Lucifer's ears.

The Prince leaned toward Abraham and Sarah. "I'm going to let you in on a little-known fact about the human body, which I personally designed," the Prince whispered. "A human baby in the womb is surrounded by a membrane which keeps out *all* blood from the mother. The child is nourished by the mother's body, but not one drop of blood from the mother ever touches the developing baby."

"One thing that means is that the baby's blood begins to develop only after the father's contribution. Biologically, the bloodline of a human is determined by the father."[6]

The Prince drove his point home, "The threat to our nation's bloodline is from *men* from outside our nation having intimate relations with our women. If that happens, their children will be in the bloodline of the outsiders. Circumcise your sons as a sign to our women. Protect our Royal bloodline!"

Abraham and Sarah nodded, understanding as well as they could. A few days later, Isaac was circumcised, as they had been instructed.

The Prince, his father and the Prime Minister met with Michael and Gabriel for a progress update in the great kingdom hall conference room.

"I could not have made it clearer," said the Prince. "Those who join themselves with enemies of the kingdom are essentially joining with prostitutes. Circumcision is their unmistakable reminder to marry only within our Royal nation."[7]

Gabriel spoke, "Point of clarification sir?"

"Of course," responded the Prince.

"You asked them to circumcise all the men in their *household*. You know that includes servants who are not from your Royal bloodline. Wouldn't that expose the bloodline to outside contamination, depending on where the servants came from?"

"Very observant, Gabriel," the Prince responded. "My instructions regarding circumcision *did* leave an apparent exposure, but that will not change the outcome."

The Prince glanced at the closed door and lowered his voice. "What I am about to say stays in this room—the success of the Immigration Project does *not* hinge on human efforts in keeping the Royal bloodline clean."[8]

Gabriel and Michael exchanged a glance.

The Prince continued. "Did you hear that little 'secret' I shared with Abraham and Sarah, about the father's part in the bloodline? *That* is key to the *entire* Immigration

Project—if a father's blood is pure Royal, then his child's blood is pure Royal, no matter what else may lurk in the mother's bloodline."

"And that is the key to the success of the Immigration Project because ...?" Gabriel trailed off.

"Because the One, or the Crusher, as Lucifer likes to call him, will *not* have a human being for a father."

Gabriel looked at the Prince, then the PM, then back to the Prince.

"Gabriel," the Prince whispered, "Crusher's mother—she will be a *virgin!*"[9]

Gabriel whispered back, "But how ...?

The Prince glanced at the Prime Minister, who winked but said nothing.

Lessons of Loyalty

When Abraham circumcised Isaac and the rest of the men in his household, the King's Academy had effectively put up a fence between their campus and the rest of the earth. The Prince was fully aware that this separation would make his nation even more of a target than ever. He knew that to withstand Lucifer's attacks, his new nation needed strong leadership, leadership that was completely loyal to the kingdom.

"You have chosen these people for the most difficult task imaginable," the PM said to the Prince.

"They need to know that they are up to the challenge," the Prince responded, "and Abraham will demonstrate what it means to be loyal to the kingdom."

Abraham was the Prince's chosen leader but his loyalty had never been tested to the limit. Even he didn't know for certain how total his allegiance was to the King.

"Humans are nothing more than self-centered animals that walk on two feet," Lucifer explained to his officers. "Loyalty to anything outside of themselves is beyond their comprehension. I have seen too many self-absorbed and foolish humans to think otherwise."

"Let's show everyone what my man Abraham is made of," the Prince said, as he stepped out to meet him.

"Abraham, as the founding father of my nation, I want you to offer up your son Isaac as your substitute for kingdom justice," the Prince announced. "He fits the criteria—he is *innocent*, he is *willing* to do whatever you ask of him, and he is *from your household*, your only son. Take him up on the hilltop and offer him up as your substitute, so your kingdom record will be clean."

"Game over," thought Lucifer. "There is no way he'll go through with this."

Abraham set out to do exactly what the Prince had commanded, in exactly the way he was told to do it. On a hilltop in what would later be called Jerusalem, Abraham gripped the knife with both hands and raised it over his son. He closed his eyes, gritted his teeth, and suddenly the Prince called out, "Abraham, stop! Now everyone knows you are totally loyal to the kingdom. Let Isaac go."[1]

"Whoa!" Lucifer was seriously taken aback. "So they really *can* use that free will of theirs to act for the kingdom, in spite of themselves. At least this one can."

"Don't worry," Lucifer said to his lieutenants, "we still have plenty of humans to work with. Let's just stick to the plan and in the end, the Prince may wind up with a handful of humans, but the rest will be mine."

"He didn't hold back anything from you, Father," the Prince said proudly. "He trusted you to the limit."

"Now that's what I'm talking about!" said the PM. "The man is an all-out kingdom patriot. You've chosen the right man to establish your nation!"

In time, the man who came to personify the Prince's nation was Abraham's grandson, Isaac's son, Jacob. He earned a reputation for being aggressive and contentious. Once, he even physically wrestled the Prince himself to the ground, demanding special kingdom privileges. Jacob was a handful, but the Prince respected him. The Prince told him, "You deserve a more descriptive name, so I am going to call you 'Israel,' meaning, 'he struggles with the King.'"

As a child struggles to accept a parent's authority, the Royal family on earth struggled with the authority of the Prince. Knowing they would struggle even more as they attended the King's Academy, the Prince decided that "Israel" was also an appropriate name for his nation.[2]

Up in the throne room, the Royal Father said to the Prince, "Nice wrestling match, son. It looks like that nation of yours has a lot of spunk," he grinned.

"That she does," replied the Prince, as he brushed the dust of the earth from his smiling face.

The first aspect of Lucifer's plan was in full swing. All his soldiers were keeping an eye out for the arrival of the Crusher.

Secondly, a number of his soldiers were contributing to the human bloodline again, although circumcision was clearly slowing their direct assault on Israel.

To compensate for that, Lucifer's soldiers adjusted their tactics, focusing more on embracing women outside of Israel. There were a lot more of them, and this way, Lucifer could participate in the broadest segment of the human bloodline, worldwide.

Once Lucifer's soldiers made their DNA contributions, all they had to do was help mankind understand the benefits of promiscuity, multiple sexual partners, and the self-fulfillment that these all bring. The worldview that they were promoting became the force multiplier of Lucifer's plan, making every lusty man and woman on earth his partner.

Within a few generations, virtually all the men in the nations surrounding Israel became prospective Royal bloodline hijackers. Lucifer was confident that given a little time, human nature would prevail, even in the kingdom's nation on earth.

The third aspect of Lucifer's plan was also going well. Most humans continued to focus on living well and being the best at what they did. They kept their primary attention on living the successful life, and consequently had little time to even think about the kingdom.

While all this was going on, Lucifer continued prowling the earth, always looking for ways to stay on top of the situation.[3]

The lower waiting room was servicing a steady influx of guests awaiting final judgment, and the kingdom citizens' arrival lounge was filling somewhat more slowly. The Prince wished all the citizens of earth would show interest in becoming kingdom citizens, but he had always maintained, "No one is going to be forced into the kingdom."

With twelve sons, Abraham's grandson Jacob (or Israel as he was known to many) did his part in expanding the Royal family on earth. However, Joseph, the youngest of Jacob's sons, was not well liked by his brothers.

"I have this sense," Joseph would often tell his brothers, "that you will all bow down to me someday."

His brothers were sick of Joseph and his delusions of grandeur, but Jacob said nothing to correct his youngest son. One day, Jacob sent Joseph to bring lunch to his brothers in the field.

"This is our chance," the brothers agreed, "let's kill him and make it look like an accident." Fortunately for Joseph, a caravan approached from over the hill, loaded with goods to sell in Egypt. After a quick negotiation, the traders exchanged some coins for Jacob's son, who was now headed for the Egyptian slave market.

His brothers, at last rid of "the boy who would be king," told their father Jacob his youngest son had been killed by a wild animal. Jacob was devastated.

"This is just too easy," Lucifer thought. "A little jealousy amongst brothers and these humans will destroy their would-be nation faster than I could do it myself. It's Cain and Abel all over again."

As he had promised his father, the Prince never lost sight of Joseph. The Prince orchestrated one unlikely event after another, and Joseph went from slave to prison inmate to Prime Minister of Egypt, reporting directly to Pharaoh.

When a famine hit their nation, Joseph's brothers and their families sought relief from starvation. They traveled to Egypt without any idea that Joseph was there. Joseph was surprised to see that the ones who had sold him into slavery didn't even recognize him. Keeping himself disguised, he had his brothers tell their life stories. He asked questions and his brothers shamefully admitted that long ago they had effectively murdered their little brother. Joseph saw their remorse and hopelessness, and revealed himself. Their little brother was now effectively "back from the dead." With warm embraces, Joseph welcomed them into Egypt and out of the famine. Using the authority of his position, Joseph provided food and shelter in Egypt for their entire nation.

"That was pure evil, what you did to me," Joseph told his brothers afterward. "But the Prince used it all for the good of his nation. He sent me ahead to prepare a place for you. That Prince certainly has got us covered."[4]

Centuries passed. Long after Joseph and his brothers had died, Egypt was swarming with Israelites. The new King of Egypt, who never knew Joseph, was feeling the pressure. There were so many ethnic Israelites who refused to assimilate by marrying Egyptian men and women.

"They are a threat to Egypt," whispered Lucifer, standing right next to Pharaoh, just out of sight, one dimension removed.

"The Israelites are a threat to Egypt," Pharaoh explained to his ministers, who were in complete agreement. "Round them all up and let's turn them from a threat to an asset. Let them serve Egypt as forced labor."[5]

Lucifer couldn't help but laugh, "The Prince's Royal family rounded up like cattle, and being worked like donkeys."

The Royals were not surprised at all by this turn of events. The lessons of good and evil were being learned by repetition, and they would continue to repeat throughout Israel's time at the King's Academy.

"I hope they'll pick up on the lesson," the Prime Minister said to the Prince, "When Cain murdered his brother, you drove him away to a place where Lucifer rules and where crops wouldn't grow.[6] Now, Jacob's sons practically murder their brother, and crop failure drove them into slavery under Pharaoh."

"However long it takes," the Prince said, "I'll be with them."

The Prince had told Abraham long ago that his nation would be slaves for 400 years. Now, after 430 years in the pressure cooker, Israel was about to see the Prince demonstrate his loyalty, buy back his people, and make them a free nation again.[7]

The nation of slaves grew until their numbers rivaled that of the Egyptians. Lucifer had gotten wind that the Prince planned to free his nation from Egypt by sending someone to rescue them. "Could this be the Crusher?" he wondered.

"Just look out your window," Lucifer whispered to Pharaoh, "You are about to lose control of your kingdom to those Israelite hordes."

Lessons of Loyalty

"I have to stop this menace," Pharaoh thought. He called in his advisors and issued a decree that every boy born in an Israelite family in Egypt should be thrown in the Nile to drown.

"Whatever it takes to crush the Crusher," mused Lucifer. "Help for Israel is *not* on the way."

Under the protective hand of the Prince, an Israelite baby boy named Moses was spared from the infanticide. As with Noah over a thousand years earlier, little Moses was carried to safety in a homemade boat and ultimately adopted by the daughter of the Pharaoh.[8]

As with Joseph, the Prince had plans for Moses to rescue Israel, but unfortunately, Moses took matters into his own hands, killing an Egyptian. Frightened, he fled across the border from Egypt into Arabia, to a land called Midian. Moses settled in, married a local girl and started a family. He thought he had escaped, but forty years later, the Prince caught up with him.

"There he is, tending his sheep in Midian." the PM said to the Prince as they looked down through the Crystal Sea portal.

"My people have waited long enough," said the Prince. Turning to a nearby kingdom engineer, the Prince said, "Open up a dimensional wormhole down to earth, right there," he said, pointing to Moses. "Just behind that bush so we won't blind him, but he'll know it's us."

"Yessir," the engineer replied. "Right away."

Even though this wormhole burrowed through all the dimensions of the universe, the light coming from the throne room into the desert was blinding. The branches of the large bush scattered most of the throbbing light.

The Prince spoke from the top floor of heaven, through the bush.[9] "Moses! For your own safety, don't come any closer! I am the Prince of the Royal family in the kingdom of heaven. I am the one who was with Abraham, Isaac, and

Jacob hundreds of years ago. I have heard the urgent calls for help from my people, and I will rescue them, Moses, through you. *You* will be the one to bring Israel out of Egypt into freedom."

Moses was understandably skeptical. He responded with a litany of questions and reasons why he was not the right man for the job. The Prince addressed each one, never wavering; "Moses, *you* are going to lead Israel to freedom. All the resources of my kingdom are available to support you. Kingdom soldiers will stand behind you, giving power and authority to words you will speak to Pharaoh."

"That is exactly the problem," explained Moses. "I am not a very good speaker. You really want someone who is eloquent, someone who ..."

"Moses, *stop!*" The Prince, clearly frustrated, turned for a moment and saw the Prime Minister and the King each suppressing a smile, but they immediately looked very serious when the Prince looked at them. The Prince took a deep breath, turned, and with the patience of a parent addressing a toddler, said slowly, "Moses, I will send your brother Aaron with you, and I will teach you both what to say and do."

Finally agreeing, Moses sent his wife and sons to stay with her father, and he left for Egypt. He met with Aaron, and together they met with the leaders of Israel to discuss what the Prince had planned.

Pharaoh refused to yield to Moses and Aaron's demand of freedom for the people of the kingdom. This was in spite of several displays of shock and awe from the kingdom's armed forces, which Moses called down on Egypt—death and destruction with pinpoint accuracy, killing Egyptians and destroying their infrastructure. The Israelites were unharmed by the carnage which somehow made Pharaoh's resolve stronger.

"I told your fathers that these people would be trouble," Lucifer whispered to Pharaoh. "Was I right or what? If you let them go, your legacy will be one of capitulation and shame. Think what people will say about you. *Tighten your grip, man!*"

The Prince told Moses, "Time to pull out all the stops. I will send the destroyer from the kingdom's Special Forces tonight to kill the firstborn male in every household, Israelite and Egyptian. Remember, Moses," the Prince instructed, "it's all about finding the willing and acceptable substitute from your household to take your place. This time is no different. Go tell the Israelites how the Prince had already provided their substitute and it is in their animal pen. Tell the people in every household to kill a young animal from their flock and paint the door of their homes with its blood. That will prove to the destroyer that the death sentence has already been carried out, and he will pass over their house."

There was a mad scramble by the Israelites to get their families together and safely locked indoors. The animals were slaughtered and their blood was painted on the door of every home where the Prince's people lived.

That evening at midnight, the gates along the border of the kingdom swung silently as the kingdom Special Forces deployed the destroyer across the border into the lower frontier. He visited every house in Egypt and executed every firstborn male. The kingdom expatriates of Israel huddled in their homes, hearing one scream after another from the houses of the Egyptians, as the destroyer did his work. Whenever he saw the blood painted on the door, he passed over and the household was spared.[10]

The next morning, Pharaoh, with his country still reeling from the assault, practically threw the Israelites out of Egypt.

The nation of Israel, two million strong, followed the Prince out of Egypt. He led them personally from within a gigantic towering cloud. As they marched into the night, following the Prince, the cloud switched modes and became a towering torch, providing light for the road ahead, so they could travel by day or night.[11]

The Prince looked up through the portal and grinned. As promised, he was setting the captive nation free. Smiling broadly, the King and the Prime Minister each gave him a salute.

Lucifer saw the wilderness where the Prince's nation was heading and said, "This will be a good place for them to die." After giving Pharaoh a few days to reflect on his failures, Lucifer went to offer a suggestion on how he might salvage his dignity.

It dawned on Pharaoh exactly what he had just allowed to happen. Almost every farm and public works project in Egypt had ground to a halt for lack of slave labor. On top of their devastating death toll, Pharaoh now had a political crisis. He couldn't live with the Israelites, and he couldn't live without them.

Pharaoh knew that nothing could bring back the firstborn of Egypt who had died, but he could certainly bring back those slaves. He reversed his position and sent the army of Egypt to round up the Israelites and bring them back into slavery.[12]

Egyptian horses and chariots thundered through the wilderness, ready to capture or crush the Prince's people. As Lucifer was fond of saying, "Whatever it takes."

The nation of Israel huddled on a wide beach on the Gulf of Aqaba. Water to the east, steep mountains to the north and south, and a narrow pass through the rocky wilderness on the west—and the Egyptians were about to pour through that pass onto the beach. Israel was trapped. Ten miles to the east, across the water, Moses could see the

Lessons of Loyalty

mountains of Midian in Arabia, where his wife and children waited for his return; so close yet so out of reach. He looked up at the towering cloud as if to say, "Well?"

The windows in the great kingdom hall were crowded with heavenly beings peering down through the Crystal Sea, and it was elbow to elbow outside along the banks of the sea as well. They were all watching intently as the best technology of earth threw itself against the kingdom war machine. Except for the Royals themselves, none of those gathered around the portal were sure of the Prince's next steps, but none of them had any doubts about the outcome.

"Moses!" the Prince commanded from the cloud. "Lead my nation through the sea, into freedom!"

Moses turned to the sea as the Prince deployed a team from the kingdom Corps of Engineers. They scrambled across the border into the lower frontier. They fired up an east wind and let it rip all night across the Gulf of Aqaba, creating two walls of water with a dry path down the middle. All the while, the tower of fire held back the Egyptian army.[13]

The besieged nation moved forward on the new path beneath the surface of the sea, and came up above the water, a free nation. As the last of the nation of Israel was coming up onto the shore of the Arabian wilderness, the Prince removed the tower of fire, allowing a hot pursuit by the Egyptian army.

As the Egyptians charged down the path through the sea, a kingdom engineer flipped off the wind allowing the waters to close over the army of Egypt, who marched on into Lucifer's lower waiting room, to wait for the final judgment.

Along the shores of the Crystal Sea of heaven, spontaneous applause and cheering erupted. The King and the Prime Minister had big smiles on their faces as they watched from the throne room. "That is just awesome!"

said the Prime Minister. "Going under the water as slaves, and coming up into freedom."

"Awesome indeed," said the King.

Watching as the waters of the Red Sea swallowed up the Egyptian army, Lucifer remembered his own exit from heaven through the Crystal Sea, and thought, "How I hate those Royals."

A messenger approached and handed Lucifer a note. His lips curled into an evil smile as he read about the crush of soggy human beings jamming the entrance to the lower waiting room.

Law School
୨୦୦୧

With all the excitement of their escape through the sea behind them, the days in the desert were mundane by comparison. The needs and concerns of everyday life took center stage. The Prince knew exactly what his nation needed.

He showed Moses where to find water, and calling upon the logistics branch of the kingdom army, the Prince ordered up "meals for a million," a pre-dawn airdrop onto their camp, six days a week, with a double delivery on Fridays.

The kingdom army dropped tons and tons of what looked like bread flakes, onto the camp every day. By coincidence, the Israelites gave it the same name as the kingdom army had given it. They called it *manna*, which was the Israelite word for "What is this stuff?"[1]

For three long months after crossing the sea, the Prince led Moses and the nation through a barren land. Without the airdrops of manna, they would have undoubtedly starved. Finally, the nation set up camp at the base of Mount Sinai, in the rugged Arabian wilderness.[2]

The Royal Father rose from his throne. Stepping down into heaven's Crystal Sea, he personally descended to the top of Mount Sinai, covering himself, and the top of the mountain, with thick dark clouds, smoke and thunder. It was terrifying, yet the people couldn't take their eyes off it.

A voice boomed out, "Moses! Come up here!"

Moses headed up the mountainside alone and was soon surrounded by thick smoke, which got brighter with each step. Surprisingly, it did not cause him to choke.

"That's far enough Moses," the King said, still hidden from view.

"I can't see you," Moses called out.

"No you can't. It would kill you to see me as I am.[3] Sit down Moses, we have a lot to talk about, my friend."

For forty days, the patriarch of the Royal family of the kingdom met with the patriarch of the Royal family on earth. They talked. They laughed. They wept. The King shared with Moses like he had never shared with any man before. In a way, it was like the time the Prince spent in the garden with Adam, getting to know one another, camping out together, bonding with each other.[4]

"Moses, I want these people to know and remember that they are my Royal family on earth," the King explained. "These people are my treasure."[5]

After forty days together, the King handed Moses a flat stone, which he had inscribed himself. "Moses," the King said, "these are the ten foundational laws of the kingdom.[6] I know you know the prime directive; *Total allegiance to the King*. These laws provide a bit more detail, like a guide for daily living. If you find yourself disregarding any of these, you'll know you are disregarding the prime directive."

Law School

> **THE TEN FOUNDATIONAL LAWS OF THE KINGDOM**
> 1. GIVE TOTAL ALLEGIANCE TO THE KING (THE PRIME DIRECTIVE)
> 2. COMMIT TO NOTHING OR NO ONE, MORE THAN TO THE KING
> 3. NEVER CARELESSLY UTTER THE KING'S NAME, HE IS LISTENING
> 4. TAKE OFF WORK ONE DAY EACH WEEK, AND HONOR THE KING
> 5. HONOR AND RESPECT YOUR PARENTS
> 6. DO NOT MURDER
> 7. DO NOT HAVE SEX OUTSIDE OF MARRIAGE
> 8. DO NOT STEAL
> 9. DO NOT LIE
> 10. DO NOT SET YOUR HEART ON THINGS THAT BELONG TO OTHERS

Moses brought the ten laws down the mountain to find that the people of Israel had been busy breaking most of them for the forty days he was up on the mountain with the King.[7]

"This is perfect," thought Lucifer. "With these statutes in place, we'll have all the proof we need that these people are *constantly* violating the prime directive. They'll know for a fact that they can *never* be good enough to be part of the Royal family!"

The Prince and Gabriel had been watching from the throne room as the King met on the mountaintop with Moses. "If the people follow those laws, it will be really good for your nation," Gabriel noted.

The Prince nodded but said nothing.

"Of course you know that not one of your people will be able to keep *all* of those laws," he added. "Not even close."

"Precisely," the Prince responded. "The humans know it too. With these statutes in place, it will be obvious to them that they are constantly violating the kingdom's prime directive. They'll know for a *fact* that they can *never* be good enough to meet the minimum standards of kingdom citizenship."[8]

"Unless …?" Gabriel guessed something was coming.

"*Unless*," the Prince declared, "they can get their kingdom records cleared by the qualified substitute!"

"Knew it," Gabriel thought. "The Immigration Project just continues to unfold."

For centuries, most of the Israelites had known the principle of kingdom justice that allowed their punishment to be absorbed by their animals. So the laws which Moses brought them really *did* turn out to be a helpful guide for living, and not just a depressing list of unattainable values.

Even in the desert, families in Israel kept their kingdom record clean as best they could. They regularly offered up the lifeblood of a goat or lamb from their household in place of their own lives, keeping ahead of kingdom justice.

The Prince saw that of the two million people in the nation, there were thousands of households, each understanding kingdom justice in their own way, and not always getting it right. Petty arguments developed between families over the minutia of the right way to offer up the substitute, and how best to follow the laws which had been given to Moses. It was time for the kingdom Department of Justice to open a branch office at the King's Academy.

"We are going to provide my nation with a clear and consistent approach on how to clear their kingdom record of all the charges against them," the Prince explained to Moses. "I don't want anyone to be consumed with questions like, 'Is my kingdom record *really* cleared? Am I *really* free from the death penalty?'"

Moses didn't know exactly what the Prince was planning, but he knew a solution was desperately needed. He told the Prince, "Too many people have simply given up, saying, 'We can't know *exactly* what the Prince wants, so why bother? We'll deal with it on the judgment day.'"

"I know," said the Prince. "I will make it so clear how to get right with kingdom law, that the only ones who won't be cleared of their condemnation are the ones who simply don't care."

"Here are the plans for your new 'portable Justice Center,'" the Prince said to Moses, handing him a detailed list of specifications. "This Justice Center will move with you until you are established in your national homeland."[9]

"I don't think I need to tell you, Moses, how busy this portable Justice Center will be. With over a million people in Israel, the Justice Center will need to be staffed by a judiciary that is hard working and well educated in the laws of the kingdom."

"Who do you have in mind for that?" Moses asked, not wanting to be assigned even one more task.

"Remember, Moses, that night in Egypt, when I spared all the firstborn sons of Israel from the destroyer?"

Moses nodded, not sure where the Prince was going.

"I spared Israel's firstborn sons, and they literally owe their lives to me. In effect, I bought them for the kingdom. Today I am trading those I have bought, for the entire clan of Levi, your brother Aaron's family, all twenty thousand of them. These "Levites" will be Israel's judiciary, the staff of the kingdom Justice Center."[10]

The Prince went on, sounding a bit like an accountant. "I've got 273 more firstborn than you've got Levites, so you can make up the difference to me in silver, five shekels for each of the extra firstborns. Aaron will take that money to fund the startup of the Justice Center."

"No rounding it off and just calling it even?" Moses half joked at the Prince's attention to detail.

The Prince looked at Moses and responded, "No one gets rounded off or falls through the cracks in kingdom justice. Everyone is accounted for."

"Sounds good to me," Moses said.

"Me too," replied the Prince with a teacher's smile.

The deal was done. The team of Levites, as the judiciary was called, constructed the Justice Center in accordance with the detailed instructions the Prince had given Moses, and put the Justice Center into operation. Now the kingdom Justice Center was the one place the nation of Israel could come to have their kingdom records cleared.

"You are going to have to do better than that!" Lucifer said, in an imaginary conversation with the Prince. "Thirty seconds after one of those people gets their record cleared at the Justice Center, they are back in the real world. There, every one of them violates one or another of your laws almost constantly."

Lucifer went through the logic for himself. "These people forget that their exoneration at the Justice Center is only for their *past* violations, not for what they do right *after* their record gets cleared. Kingdom justice doesn't care if it's a million violations or just that one which they committed since having their record cleared — they still get death."

Thinking about it, Lucifer was convinced there was more to the puzzle. "I'm sure the King plans to get around the issue of 'future violations' by ensuring that Crusher is somehow *above* the dimension of time, making his substitution valid for all time. But he's still got to be a descendant of the woman in the garden, a human in the Prince's Royal bloodline."

"I just need to stick to the plan," Lucifer concluded. "If we can dominate the human bloodline, Crusher will be disqualified from clearing anybody's kingdom record. Nice try, Prince! All your people are still doomed!"

The Prince was one dimension above, but only a few feet away from Lucifer, so he heard the entire one-sided rant. The Prince said to himself, "If you only knew the power of the kingdom, you little snake."[11]

The nation had been at the foot of Mount Sinai for almost eleven months. Add to that the three months since they passed through the Red Sea and they had spent as much time in the wilderness as Noah and his family spent with the animals in the Ark.

"Time to pack up and head out," the Prince told Moses. "I have prepared a place for you."

As fast as two million people and all their belongings can move, the nation of Israel headed north. With this land only a few short weeks away, the people still found things to complain about. They were tired of the snake and scorpion infested wilderness and eating the same food every day. Moses sometimes felt he had only one nerve left, and these people were stepping on it. Frustrated, he told the Prince, "I'd rather be dead than have this job."[12]

Lucifer grinned broadly when he heard that. "These people have gone from being slaves of Pharaoh to being slaves of the Prince," he said to his lieutenant. "Moses is dragging them through the desert and the Prince only provides enough food to keep them from rioting. That Prince is as close to losing the people as he is to losing their leader, and that's fine with me."

The Prince worked with Moses and held the nation together until they approached Canaan (roughly twenty-first century Israel), the land that the Prince had promised to them.

Moses sent scouts ahead into Canaan. They reported that before Israel could settle into the land, they would first have to evict the current residents—giants—descendants of the Nephilim![13]

Even though the Prince had assured Moses that the current inhabitants were not to be feared, everybody seemed to have their own opinion. Ten out of the twelve scouts warned that Israel would be massacred if they went forward into Canaan. Joshua and Caleb were the lone dissenters, encouraging Israel to follow Moses and the Prince, but they were shouted down by the crowds.[14] The nation refused to budge and even got ready to pelt Moses with rocks.

The Prince was livid. He pulled Moses aside. "Are these people blind as well as stupid? Since they left Egypt I've proven that I can deliver them through *anything*, but they believe the lies of the warlord instead of my promises. I'm ready to kill them all now and start over again with you!"[15]

Moses, exhibiting an uncharacteristic calm said, "Now Prince, if you do that, you know that word will get back to Egypt, and you will be known as the Prince who couldn't lead his people out of a sandbox, so he killed them."[16]

"*Fine*," said the Prince, "I won't force *anyone* into a life of prosperity. You can all wander around in the desert until every one of the adults in your nation is dead! Joshua and Caleb are the only exceptions, since they stood for me and my kingdom. When every other adult is dead, then we can try again."[17]

"This is not so bad," Moses thought, having just influenced the Prince to spare his people.

"This is not so bad," the Prince thought, "Moses is really maturing as a leader. He is beginning to act as if he cares for these people, even when they are contentious beyond reason."

"This is not so bad," Lucifer thought, pleased at seeing how easily the people chose his advice over the Prince's.

"Looks like the Kings Academy will be extending into extra sessions," the Prince said to the Prime Minister.

"Sometimes the only lessons these humans really learn are the hard ones," the PM responded. "A few more years in the desert and perhaps the lessons of kingdom loyalty will really sink in."

Once again, Israel picked up and marched into the desert. This time, however, it was away from the land that the Prince had promised to give them.

For the next forty years, the nation wandered through the desert, being led and fed under the direction of the Prince. The portable Justice Center was in full operation and the people made a regular practice of getting their kingdom records cleared. Israel finally reached the Jordan River, across from Canaan, the same land into which the Prince had tried to lead them before.

The Prince and the Prime Minister came to Moses. The Prince told him, "Moses! You're 120 years old. Your time as Israel's leader is up. You were the right man for the job of getting the people out of slavery and taking them through law school, but no further."

"You must be joking," Moses stammered. "I've led these people for more than forty years. I've followed all your laws..." The Prince listened with genuine compassion to his friend who began to choke up. "I worked so hard—doesn't that count for anything? At least let me bring them across the border."

"I can't, my friend," the Prince spoke softly. "In the desert, remember?" Moses was silent. "Two million people, dying from thirst—they had their eyes glued on you. Aaron called them together to see for themselves how I would provide for them. They *knew* what was going to happen. All you had to do was command the rock like I told you, and I would make water pour from it—more than enough for everybody. They were straining to hear you speak those words—but instead you bashed the rock with your staff."[18]

"Yes, and water came out!" Moses pleaded. "Please, let me lead them across the border."

"Enough![19] You're not getting it, are you? Yes, water came out. My people were thirsty, Moses—of course I gave them water. The point is, you disrespected me in front of my people. Two million of my own family watched as you consciously ignored what I told you to do. No, you're not going to lead them in—and no, we're not going to discuss this anymore. Turn over your leadership to Joshua."[20]

An old man, Moses died within sight of the land that the Prince had selected for his family's homeland.

General Michael led a kingdom military honor guard to carry Moses out of his body to the kingdom citizens' arrival lounge. A group of Lucifer's soldiers watched from a safe distance. They were frustrated after years of watching Moses hide behind the Prince's protection. Just as the kingdom honor guard was leaving, Lucifer's soldiers stepped quietly toward the lifeless human body of Moses, and were about to bring it to their General as a trophy. Michael turned and swung his massive sword, clipping but not killing the vandals. He shouted, "Back off! Don't you *ever* touch the body of an honorary kingdom citizen. Especially this one!" They jumped back and scurried away.[21]

Moses was met at the entrance of the lounge by Abraham, as well as a number of his friends from the past forty years in the desert. As he settled in, a lounge attendant approached him and said, "Message for you sir," handing Moses an envelope. He opened it to find a hand-written note on Royal letterhead …

Moses –

Meet me later on the mountaintop with Elijah. I want to talk with you about bringing <u>everybody</u> across the border.

– Prince

Moses had no idea what the note meant. He exchanged a glance with Abraham who smiled, but would say nothing about it.[22]

School of Government
ஒ~ஒ

Moses' longtime assistant Joshua had assumed leadership and was ready to take Israel into the homeland which the Prince had chosen. They were certain to face opposition, but Joshua had learned at least one thing: when the Prince says go, you *go*!

The Prince stood with Joshua and went over the instructions one more time. Waving his hand over the map, the Prince said, "From here to the Mediterranean, up to Lebanon and east to the Euphrates River in Iraq, it's all ours, just as I promised Moses. OK Joshua, let's go."[1]

"Start packing up!" Joshua shouted to his leaders. The command echoed throughout the nation.

This time there were no arguments, no talk of the fearsome natives. They were heading west toward the Jordan River, toward their new homeland in Canaan, led by Joshua who was led by the Prince.

The influence of Lucifer and his soldiers had been felt in Canaan for years by the time Joshua and the Israelites arrived. As in many other parts of the world, freewheeling sex had become socially acceptable. Prostitution had become just another way to make a living.

On their first night at camp in the new land, the Prince came to Joshua in his tent. "There is something you need to do before we go any further. While you were in the desert, a lot of the people didn't circumcise their sons as they had been instructed. You know the reason for circumcision— for a woman to know for sure if the man she marries is one of us. While you were in the desert, it was a moot point, and I let it go. You were all alone out there, but Canaan is a very different place."

Joshua could tell where this conversation was going, and he wasn't looking forward to hearing the rest of it.

"You know what needs to be done, Joshua. Protect my family."

The next day, Joshua gathered his leaders and told them what the Prince had said. They were not excited about the assignment either, but agreed it had to be done.

That week, every man that had been born during their forty years in the desert was circumcised, over 400,000 of them. From that time on, the place they had camped was known as "the hill of foreskins."[2]

After a few weeks of recovery, Joshua and the nation he led moved across Canaan to the fortified city of Jericho. Spies were sent ahead to assess the city's defenses. They befriended a local woman named Rahab, who was well known throughout Jericho as a prostitute. She made no attempt to hide this as she met in secret with the men from Israel. Word traveled fast about the visiting spies, and when the King of Jericho heard, he sent word to Rahab for her to turn them in.[3]

The King's messenger banged on the door and Rahab bought a few moments to consider her situation. "Just a minute while I get decent!" she called.

"Rahab… decent," the messenger smirked as he waited.

"These men of Israel are the first ones to speak with me in *years* who weren't undressing me first with their eyes and then with their filthy hands," she thought.

Rahab quickly made her decision and confided in the men, "The King of Jericho is scared to death of you. Everybody in the city has heard that the Prince is with Israel, and about how he took you through the sea out of Egypt. Here's the deal—I'll help you escape, but when you take this city, you've got to spare me and my family."

"Deal," said the spies. "Just be ready when we come back."

"Rahab!" came the shout along with a pounding on her door. "Bring out the spies!" called the King's messenger.

Rahab composed herself, opened the door and flashed her professional smile. "Tell the King I'm sorry," she lied to the man at the door, "The men he is looking for left town just before the city gates closed last evening."

"Well then, why don't you invite me in and we'll talk about it over a glass of wine?" the messenger asked, jingling his coin purse. His eyes were drawn to Rahab's cleavage.

"Get out of here, you pig!" Rahab spit as she slammed the door. They were both surprised at her reaction, given her well-earned reputation.

Rahab helped the spies hide on the roof of her house that night, and the following day, the spies made their getaway. Within a few days, Israel marched on Jericho. The Prince told Joshua exactly what to do. The walls of the city collapsed before their eyes and what was left of the city was burned. True to their word, the Israelites whisked Rahab and her family out of the danger zone and they were welcomed into the Prince's nation.

"Welcome Rahab!" Lucifer shouted with glee. "I *love* it when a prostitute joins the Royal family! Descendants of my human children have been living it up in Canaan for a long time, so Rahab is certainly no Royal. She will carry on *my* family line inside the Prince's nation, and little baby Crusher will be *my* pride and joy—*my* legacy—*my* son!"

For decades, the Prince led his nation on a program of territorial expansion throughout Canaan. All that the Prince required was that the people give full allegiance to him, keep his laws and commands as best they could, and get their offenses cleared at the Justice Center regularly.

As needed, the Prince provided resources from the army of heaven to fight their battles for them. More than once, however, the people disregarded the Prince's instructions, and then the Prince would stand-down. Usually that meant Israel would get crushed for lack of kingdom air support.

Two steps forward, one step back. Slowly, the nation of Israel spread out and settled throughout Canaan.

No matter how often the nation turned its back on the Prince, and went their own way, the Levites kept the fires burning at the Justice Center, day in, day out. Anyone who wanted to get right with the kingdom knew that was the one place to do it.

With the passing of Joshua, the Prince appointed one man after another to act as his representative to the people. But on the whole, the nation's attention seemed to be sliding away from the kingdom. The people told Samuel, the Prince's current representative, that they wanted the Prince to give them a *real* king, a *human* king, like the other countries had.

Lucifer understood. "They want a *real* leader, not some being from another dimension who they seldom, if ever, see. Even the Prince's nation is coming around," he thought.

The Prince listened quietly as Samuel explained the people's demands for a human king. Finally, the Prince responded with a note of sorrow in his voice, "These people do not even remember why I made them separate from the rest of the nations, or why I told them over and over to protect their bloodline! They circumcise their own sons, and they don't even know why. They think it's about hygiene, or that it protects them from diseases or something! They've forgotten they are royalty. They have forgotten *every* provision of mine, and *every* battle I have fought and won for them!"

Samuel said, "They just want a strong man to look up to, one who will tell them what they need to do ..." His voice trailed off, realizing the rejection that the Prince must be feeling. Samuel felt he had let down both the Prince and the people.

"Samuel," the Prince said quietly, "don't take this on yourself. These people are not rejecting your leadership. They are rejecting mine.[4] They don't understand what human government is like. It is time for our nation to attend the school of government.

Samuel sighed. He knew that there were no easy classes at the King's Academy.

The Prince said, "Tell them that their request will be granted. In the King's Academy school of government, they will learn from firsthand experience, exactly what it means to have a human king over them." He went into detail, "Tell them a human king will draft their sons into his army and force them to run into enemy fire. He'll conscript their sons and daughters to work in his own personal businesses and munitions factories. He and his friends will take the best of the peoples personal production and on top of that, you can all expect a 10% tax on everything you have.[5]

"Samuel," said the Prince, "every single human government is like this, to one extent or another, not just the king I will give them. The one thing I want my people to learn in the school of government is the difference between a kingdom government and a human government. You've seen how *I* rule and protect my nation. Now you'll learn by experience that all human governments wind up crushing their own people to one extent or another."[6]

"Samuel, remind them that I *want* to be their King, but they rejected me.[7] But so they don't despair, also remind them that I will continue to protect this rebellious, forgetful, and ungrateful nation, all the way through King's Academy graduation, and beyond."

Lucifer was quite satisfied that things were going his way. These people certainly weren't acting like they were the Royal family on earth. They acted exactly like everyone else. And now that the Prince had granted their request to be under a human king, they were back in slavery.

With his officers surrounding him, Lucifer gloated, "The Prince's whole protect-the-bloodline thing is dead, too. They just can't resist those foreign women. *None* of them can claim to be a Royal any more! And circumcision…! Nice try, Prince! It didn't work. You can put that ritual in the museum!"[8]

"Even the prostitute Rahab from Jericho is now a matriarch in the Prince's human family, and that makes me a patriarch![9] Talk about a mixed-up family tree!" Lucifer cackled. "I say, put 'em all to death, let us all into the kingdom, or be a hypocrite!"

Lucifer was content, sure that the Prince's plan was a feeble, doomed attempt to win the affection and loyalty of these spineless, stupid, and self-centered humans. "And if that glorious substitute of his ever shows up, the Prince is going to be the one to get crushed, not me."[10]

Lucifer was confident that the Prince had misplaced his eggs in the flimsy basket of a pure Royal bloodline. Delighted at how his plan was falling into place, he shouted, "That bloodline isn't Royal anymore, Prince, and it certainly isn't pure, unless my boys and I are pure royalty!"

4: Reclaiming the Earth
Kingdom Head of State Arrives

On the top floor conference room, the King, the Prime Minister, and the Prince spoke excitedly about the Prince's upcoming trip across the border to earth.

This trip was not going to be a down-and-back hop through the Crystal Sea into some pasture of earth. This was to be total immersion into a world full of good and evil not unlike what Adam and Eve experienced when they stepped out of the garden.

The Prince was going human.

General Gabriel knocked and entered the room. He bowed slightly and then said, "Is it time?"

"Let's go," said the Prince. He and the Prime Minister followed Gabriel into the Crystal Sea, stepping down to the lower frontier. In a small town called Nazareth, in northern Israel, they found the one they were looking for.

In heaven, General Gabriel has a very impressive appearance, even amongst the fiercest squadrons in the kingdom army. When he enters the three dimensions of earth, visible to humans, he is incredibly intimidating.

As gently as he could, this giant of a warrior stepped into the presence of a fourteen-year-old girl and whispered, "Greetings, Mary." Not surprisingly, the general's unexpected entrance caused her to jump, then shake with fear. "Don't be afraid!" he said gently, "I have great news for you from the King of heaven. You know about the One who has been promised by the founding fathers of Israel for centuries—the One who will free the nation of Israel from the demands of kingdom justice? That One is your son, Mary."

"B-but, I have no son! Joseph, my fiancé—we are not yet married—I have never slept with a man!" she stammered.

"I know," said Gabriel, "the Prime Minister himself, from the kingdom of heaven is here. He will deposit the life of the long-awaited One into you, Mary—and don't worry about Joseph—I will talk with him tonight. He will be your husband, and Jesus will be your son."[1]

From a dimension unseen by Mary, the Prime Minister and the Prince of heaven stepped toward her. Both of them seemed to dissolve as they approached the young girl, but only the Prime Minister emerged on the other side. The Prince of heaven had entered a human, to become a human.

The long-promised One was born in an animal pen in the small town of Bethlehem, just south of Jerusalem.

Some foreign dignitaries who had studied the writings of Israel's founding fathers, journeyed great distances to welcome the promised One.[2] On the night of his birth, however, not many were on hand to greet the Prince. Other than Mary and Joseph, Jesus was surrounded by barnyard animals and a few local shepherds.

Everyone in the kingdom, however, knew of the big event. Thousands of kingdom soldiers paraded through the sky over Bethlehem, cheering and shouting to celebrate the Royal birth. As quickly as they had appeared, they slipped

Kingdom Head of State Arrives

back into the kingdom, as if exiting through unseen doorways.[3]

Word of the birth of the One reached Lucifer quickly, and he almost choked. "What!?" he bellowed. "Tell me that again!"

The messenger stood nervously before him saying, "Bethlehem—in a stable—last night. The parents are a couple from Nazareth. I don't even think they are married. Kingdom security was tight; we could hardly get close enough to see. But we *know* it was him. It *had* to be."

It was clear that the Crusher had arrived, and his name was Jesus.

Enraged, Lucifer tore the head off the messenger, then composed himself and sat down to consider his next move.

Even after a period of reflection, Lucifer, though he appeared calm, was livid. "This One thinks he can just waltz onto my planet without consequence. The earth is still mine. Those humans gave it to me. The Prime Minister confirmed it. *I am* the legal authority here."

Though Jesus' arrival was upsetting, Lucifer knew that he still had an ace in his pocket. At the end of the day, he knew that Jesus could not qualify under kingdom law as an acceptable substitute to take the death penalty for these humans. He knew the bloodline of this Jesus wasn't Royal, and Lucifer had the genealogy of Jesus to prove it. "Thanks to good old Grandma Rahab the prostitute, and many others on both sides of Jesus' lineage, he is a citizen of earth, by birth *and* by bloodline!"

Lucifer was actually looking forward to seeing the great judge's face when he dropped *that* card on the table.

For now, however, he kept his eye on the ball that was in play. "I will crush this human king, and anyone who tries to follow him—this is war!"

Lucifer commanded his lieutenants, "Get word to the local king, Herod, that a competitor for his throne has arrived in Bethlehem. Let him know he needs to crush the Crusher. Remember last time we missed Moses in the slaughter of the newborns, so make sure Herod casts a wider net this time!"

By the time King Herod commanded the execution of all male children in the region two years old and younger, the Prime Minister had already led Joseph and his family into Egypt.[4] They stayed there until Herod and his fury had died. Then the PM led them, under the wings of a heavily armed contingent of kingdom military guards, to the backwater town of Nazareth in northern Galilee, where young Jesus learned carpentry from his stepfather Joseph.

Though Israel was under Roman occupation, Joseph, Mary and Jesus led a relatively quiet life in the sleepy town of Nazareth. A battalion of heaven's soldiers stood watch from above and did battle with Lucifer's henchmen as needed, ensuring that, at least to the humans, the Prince's early days on earth were quiet.

When Jesus was about thirty years old, he traded in the life of a carpenter and set out to do what he had come to do—become the leader of the kingdom of heaven on earth. When he started his public life, the former carpenter hammered home one message more than any other, to anyone who would listen: "The kingdom of heaven is near."

Jesus' cousin John was known to Lucifer and his underlings as a radical, a troublemaker who stirred up the people against the status quo of earth, pointing them to the Prince's kingdom. Jesus sought John out, and found him down at the Jordan River.[5] John announced, as he did every day to all who would listen: "The Prince of heaven is coming! Get ready!"

He told them that in order to get ready to gain kingdom citizenship, they needed to publicly renounce all allegiance to Lucifer, the ruler of the earth. If they did that, John would submerge them beneath the surface of the river and a moment later, lift them up. "Your life as a citizen of earth is about to be over! You are now pre-qualified for a new life as a citizen of the kingdom of heaven!"[6]

Kingdom-minded people came from all over to, as John put it, get pre-qualified for kingdom citizenship. They were not sure how it would all work out, but they sure didn't want to miss an opportunity to become part of the kingdom which had been promised for centuries.

As each person was pre-qualified by John, there was cheering that rocked the gathered crowd around the Crystal Sea outside the great kingdom hall.[7]

Jesus approached his cousin John at the Jordan River. John had already suspected his cousin's true identity. He had heard the stories from his mom and Aunt Mary, and somehow, he thought that Jesus might just be "the One." When John was asked by Jesus to be pre-qualified as a kingdom citizen, John was puzzled. Why would Jesus ask him to do that? If Jesus *was* the One, he was a kingdom citizen *already*. He didn't need to be pre-qualified. "What is going on here?" John wondered.

It wasn't about *becoming* a kingdom citizen for Jesus. John's suspicions were correct. He already *was* one. Jesus' father was a Royal from the kingdom itself, making Jesus a kingdom citizen by virtue of his bloodline. It was actually about *renouncing* his citizenship of earth.

Jesus was born in Bethlehem, making him a natural-born citizen of the earth. By birth, Jesus was legally a subject of Lucifer, the ruler of the earth. He was eligible for citizenship in both the earth *and* the kingdom of heaven. He was fully human by birth and fully Royal by blood.

Jesus explained this to his cousin, "Entry into the kingdom is restricted to citizens of the kingdom who carry kingdom passports, but dual citizenship is *not* recognized or tolerated in the kingdom.[8] If someone publicly renounces their citizenship on earth and its ruler, and commits themselves fully to the kingdom and the Royals, they are eligible for citizenship and a kingdom passport."

John just stood looking at Jesus, hip deep in the flowing water, not saying a word.

"John," Jesus whispered in his cousin's ear, "anyone who wants to be admitted to heaven *must* take a stand *for* the kingdom and *against* its enemies. It is absolutely necessary for me to publicly renounce my citizenship of earth, and along with it any authority which the warlord Lucifer wants to exercise over me because I was born here."

John didn't move.

"I *have* to do this, John," Jesus said with a quiet urgency. "I cannot take on the mantle of leadership of my Royal nation on earth, until I publicly renounce the ruler of the land of my birth."[9]

It was a lot for John to process all at once, though he knew that it had to be true. Jesus broke the tension, "Just do it, John," he winked at his cousin, "or I'll tell your mother."

In a loud voice, John led Jesus in publicly renouncing Lucifer, the ruler of the land of his birth. John lowered him under the water and Jesus came up. There was an eruption of cheering in the great kingdom hall as Jesus burst through the surface of the Jordan River, with a huge smile on his face!

Clearly excited, the Royal Father reached down from his throne and literally tore a temporary wormhole from the border of heaven right down to that stretch of the Jordan River.[10] The Father called down, and everyone gathered around Jesus and John heard it.

"My *son!* I can't *tell* you how pleased I am with you!"

With his mouth open in awe, John watched. The Prime Minister stepped down through the new opening, and with the grace of a bird, landed on Jesus.[11] As he would do again

Kingdom Head of State Arrives

many times for others in the coming years, the PM deposited a kingdom passport and full diplomatic credentials into the Prince's human body, authorizing access and authority in all dimensions through the top floor of heaven.

Prior to becoming human, the Prince had enjoyed unrestricted kingdom access, and more. Laying down that authority for the previous thirty years, and now getting it back, was exhilarating. However, as Jesus, he was about to have that authority tested and stretched by the warlord who was not about to let the kingdom muscle-in on his territory.

Unlike in the kingdom, the ruler of the earth has absolutely no problem with dual citizenship. "It's this intolerant renunciation that I can't stand," Lucifer would tell his troops. "Divided loyalties are just fine with me," Lucifer would say. "Can't we all just get along?"

Lucifer was even OK with having the Justice Center in the midst of his territory, as long as the people kept their loyalties divided. The new kingdom Justice Center in Jerusalem was so impressive that the justices in charge were more focused on maintaining their high-level jobs and social schedules, than they were on upholding the prime directive of the kingdom. "Good for *you!*" Lucifer would cheer them on. "There are a lot of things going on in your life and they're all *very* important!"[12]

Despite some such apparent victories, Lucifer knew that John and Jesus had to be dealt with. "These renunciations of me personally need to stop before things get out of hand," he thought. "I need to talk sense to Jesus."

Lucifer wouldn't have long to wait.

The voice of the Prime Minister whispered to Jesus, "It's time to tune out the distractions.[13] Your father wants to prepare you for the battle ahead. Let's head out into the desert."

For forty days, Jesus walked alone in the desert, without food, without shelter. Near the end of that time, when his human body was running on empty, Jesus had a visitor.

Emergency Summit Meeting

Lucifer considered what he would say to Jesus, and decided to take the cooperative approach. He decided not to bring up the matter of Jesus' sketchy bloodline, saving that gem for later.

"We could be partners, even friends. The Prince wants the earth and its people; I've got the earth and its people. It's my earth and I can give it to the Prince if I want. We'll work together. It's a win-win. Yeah."

Lucifer found Jesus in the desert, blistered, tired, and hungry. He certainly didn't look like kingdom royalty.[1]

"Jesus," Lucifer said with convincing sincerity, "you need to eat something. I cannot believe the Prime Minister led you out here in the desert to starve like this. Let me get you some, uh ..." He looked around. "Here, Jesus," he held out a rock, expectantly. "Just say the word and turn this into a loaf of bread. If you really are the Prince of heaven, we both know that will not be a problem."

"Bread is not enough to keep a man alive." Jesus replied. "Humans are not simply animals that eat, sleep, and die on this earth of yours."

"Of course, Jesus, of course," Lucifer said, quickly dropping the rock. "But you are right. The entire planet is mine, as a matter of fact." Lucifer led Jesus through a dimensional doorway, to a vantage point where they could see the entire earth.[2] "But in a lot of ways, it's a mess. It really does need you to straighten it out, Jesus, to rule over it. Tell you what—let me give the world to you. Here, take it; it's yours. But first, let's just go back to the river and take back what you said about renouncing me and my sovereignty. We'll set the record straight for the people. Let them know that you and I are working together. Let's—"

"*Stop!*" Jesus interrupted. "You know the prime directive of the kingdom, '*total allegiance to the King!*'"

Lucifer paused. "Yes, of course. Forgive me, Jesus. What was I thinking? The King. Yes, everyone needs, first and foremost, to know and honor the King." He took Jesus through another dimensional doorway to the top of the tallest tower of the kingdom Justice Center in Jerusalem.[3] They looked down on the people milling about at the foot of the building. "You can point these people to the Royal Father in a very powerful way, Jesus. Jump down from here, right now, in front of all these people. You know that the King would never let you get hurt. Everyone would see the kingdom soldiers save you and they would know that the Royal Father sent you. You will be the talk of Israel, and you will point them to your Father!"

"You know what happens to those who force the hand of the King, don't you? *Don't you?*" Jesus repeated, knowing full well that Lucifer knew. "It never ends well."

They stood silently looking at each other.

This meeting had not gone as Lucifer had hoped. He now knew for certain what he had suspected earlier. This was no courtesy visit from a ruler of heaven to Lucifer's earth. This was definitely an illegal invasion of his sovereign territory.

Lucifer vanished through an invisible door, muttering, "You have not heard the last of me."

Emergency Summit Meeting

A platoon of kingdom soldiers rushed through that same door, surrounding and tending to the Prince.[4]

John's pre-qualifications continued, for a while.

Lucifer knew better than most, that the humans had free will. He knew he was powerless to physically prevent them from using their free will to defect to the kingdom.

"But we can convince them that their renunciation wasn't genuine," he explained to his henchmen. "It'll be easy! They actually prove it to themselves every time they put their own interests above the kingdom's, or violate a kingdom law. When they do, we'll whisper a little reminder, *'That's* why you are not pre-approved for citizenship in heaven. Application rejected! Hah!'"

Lucifer's followers joined in with other one-liners for the humans to use on those would-be kingdom citizens:

"There is no kingdom! This world is all there is!"

"If there is a kingdom, where is it? Seeing is believing!"

"The kingdom is a fairy tale for weak minds—a crutch, a coping strategy!"

"They will believe me," thought Lucifer. "They always have." He turned and strode toward Galilee, to have a word with Herod, the puppet king of the region, about getting rid of the troublemaker John.

Herod didn't like John any more than Lucifer did. Soon, Herod ordered that the activist John be arrested, locked up, and eventually beheaded.[5] Herod didn't care much about the kingdom or those renunciations, but he was *absolutely* fed up with John frequently pointing out Herod's lifestyle to the people, publicly declaring that it was evil and anti-kingdom.

It wouldn't be the last time that Lucifer recruited the support of a local government to deal with those who encourage defection to the kingdom.

Offer of Kingdom Citizenship

The location of an announcement can be almost as important as the announcement itself. Returning to his hometown of Nazareth, Jesus went to the community leaders who greeted him warmly at the local kingdom Justice Center.[1] These men had known Jesus since he was a boy. They had watched him grow up.

"Jesus, we were just gathering for the reading from the books of Israel's founders," one of the elders told him. "Come join us—better yet, read a selection from the book for us." He handed Jesus one of the old books containing the history and wisdom of the nation of Israel.

Jesus knew that heaven's nation on earth had been waiting for hundreds, no *thousands* of years for what he was about to say. He also knew they weren't expecting it today, especially in dusty little Nazareth. He wondered how they would react.

"I would be honored." Jesus rose, took the book and stood before the leaders and a small gathering crowd. He looked about, smiling as his gaze met eye after familiar eye from his childhood days. He cleared his throat and spoke in a loud voice: "All the power of the kingdom of heaven is upon me."

They all knew Jesus was simply quoting directly from the book of Isaiah, one of Israel's founding fathers, but there was an incredible authority in his voice.[2] It was almost like it was *personal*.

Jesus continued reading, "*I* have been chosen by the King of heaven to give you a message," he paused as the audience strained with anticipation. "He has selected *me* to set free the prisoners and the oppressed. He has sent *me* to give sight to people who are too blind to see. *I* have come to heal those with broken bodies and hearts. *I* am here to announce to you that the King of heaven is now buying back the earth and his people!"

Jesus closed the book, handed it back, took his seat, and looked down. The silence got more intense.

Jesus then lifted his head and spoke again, "That long-awaited day of freedom for Israel starts right here in Nazareth, and it starts right now, *today*!" This time he was not quoting from the book, but speaking on his own.[3]

The onlookers were stunned. Some were offended.

It took a few moments before anyone could speak. One person finally whispered, his irritated voice growing in volume as he spoke, "Maybe Jesus has spoken with the Prince himself, or maybe even the King!" With a clear touch of sarcasm, he added, "What do you say, Jesus?"

A family friend of Joseph, Jesus' late father, tried to ease the tension by interjecting a compliment about Jesus' powerful delivery. "Joseph's boy sounds like a founding father himself!"

As much as he had loved his mother's husband Joseph, Jesus knew who his real father was. Turning to the sarcastic elder, he said, "You know from Israel's history that the authority of a founding father of Israel is never appreciated in his own hometown, so the King sent his representatives elsewhere. So be it with Nazareth; the wonders of the kingdom will pass you by."

Offer of Kingdom Citizenship

The leaders looked at each other, "I think he's just insulted us." The crowd's murmuring grew into sharp comments. Regrettable words were thrown. The next thing anyone knew, Jesus was being pushed by a mob toward a nearby cliff on the edge of town.

As they approached the precipice, Jesus made a slight turn into a dimension just beyond their human sight.

"Where did he go?"

"I was holding his arm and he vanished!"

"You idiots!"

Invisible to the agitated crowd, Jesus simply walked away.[4]

And so began the public declarations of Jesus. Over the next three years, he repeated the same message day after day: "The border crossing into the kingdom of heaven is about to open!"

The crowds following Jesus grew daily, making it difficult for him to keep up with all the demands on him. The Prime Minister told Jesus, "It's time to establish a team of honorary consuls, a group of men committed to you, who have pre-qualified for citizenship in heaven. We'll train them on getting the kingdom message out in a powerful way, and you will lead them by example."

Jesus knew the plan. He appointed twelve of his followers as honorary consuls for the kingdom.[5] They were not chosen for their social, intellectual or financial status. The Prince was able to just look at someone and know their character.[6] Though some of them were a bit rough around the edges, the Prince knew that these men would eventually embrace the King and the kingdom more tightly than they would embrace life itself.

Interestingly, Jesus didn't choose anyone who worked at the kingdom Justice Center, though the justices there had all heard about Jesus from their colleagues in Nazareth. They were keeping an eye on him.

Jesus gathered his honorary consuls together, "You probably don't even know what an honorary consul is. It is someone who is *not* a citizen of the kingdom but who has been authorized by the kingdom to work on its behalf. As you will soon see, my main objective is to offer kingdom citizenship to citizens of earth, and that offer will start with each of you when the time comes."

"You will hear me say over and over, how people can become citizens of heaven. When my work here on earth is done, the Prime Minister of the kingdom will visit you and give to you, and every one who is pre-qualified, a kingdom passport, authorizing full access to the kingdom."

Looking at his new honorary consuls, Jesus said, "I expect that most of you in this group, after you become citizens, will be appointed ambassadors, as well. You will then have full authority to call down all the resources of heaven as needed—but I am getting ahead of myself."

"Your main job for now as honorary consuls is to watch me and learn. We want to demonstrate to everyone in Israel, by our words and by our actions, that the kingdom is really *real*, and the kingdom is *right here!*"[7] He waved his arms at dimensions that the honorary consuls could not see. "Everything the people have heard from the founding fathers is true. I am about to make it possible for humans to enter the kingdom. Now *that* is good news! All they have to do is turn their back on the warlord Lucifer, and take the citizenship deal that is about to be offered."

Not yet sure what the citizenship deal would be, they all nodded as a crowd gathered around them.

"OK, let's get to it!" said Jesus, stepping into the crowd, to get up close and personal with humans who want to learn what the kingdom is all about.

This was the start of an almost three year "kingdom awareness tour," for Jesus and his entourage. Walking throughout Israel, Jesus met with the people face to face. It

Offer of Kingdom Citizenship

was a nonstop series of one-on-one conversations, speeches to the crowds, firm handshakes, and brotherly embraces. Most of all, though, Jesus told stories.

He would speak important truths about the kingdom of heaven in the form of simple stories.[8] The stories were simple, but it wasn't always clear exactly what his point was. At times, even his honorary consuls found themselves baffled by Jesus' stories.

"Why not just give them straight talk on the kingdom?" they asked Jesus, after the crowds had left. "Let them know exactly where it is, and exactly how to get there!"

"I don't want everyone to understand what I am saying right now," Jesus said. "What I want them to hear from me is that the kingdom is real, and it's right here, right now. I want them to hear what the kingdom is like, as compared to the earth. Then they need to think about where their own allegiances lie and what it might mean for them to give up citizenship on earth and commit to the kingdom. Not everyone is ready to embrace the kingdom."

"You've seen me heal people, and even raise some from the dead, but every one of them is still going to die," Jesus paused to let them think. "But *you*, my friends, have a greater assignment. You will invite people to live *forever* in the kingdom. That is why I speak plainly to you. You need to understand the kingdom message more clearly than anyone."[9]

While walking from one town to another, Jesus asked Peter, "What do you hear from the people? Who do they say that I am?"

"They say you're a prophet for sure. Maybe even one of the founding fathers come back to life!"

"I see," he said. "Who do you say I am, Peter?"

Peter stopped walking, looked Jesus in the eye and said, "I know you are the Prince of the kingdom of heaven."

Jesus paused, nodded and said, "I never told you that—my father did. But don't tell anyone, Peter."

Peter said, "Okay," but thought to himself, "Why not?"[10]

Those flocking to see and hear Jesus were a cross section of the culture. They were merchants and tax collectors, fishermen and prostitutes, Israelites, Romans, Greeks, Samaritans, the rich and the poor, the holy and the demon-possessed. He met with men, women, and children everywhere he went.

Something, however, was missing. Conspicuous by their absence from the crowds was any of the management or staff of the kingdom Justice Center. If they did show up, it was usually the Justice Center interns, on the fringes of the crowd, listening and taking notes for their superiors. Some of the people wondered, "If the border to the kingdom is opening, why isn't anyone from the Justice Center out here with you, Jesus? *They* are in charge of clearing our kingdom records. Are the kingdom rules changing?"

"Not at all," Jesus replied. "Everything you heard through Israel's founding fathers is exactly the same, then as now.[11] Some people, however," referring to the officials at the Justice Center, "have become more interested in being known as experts in the law, than knowing the one who gave them the law. They like being in charge more than they want to know the kingdom and the Royals."[12]

"That's it!" Lucifer realized. "Turf war!" Calling his minions together, they mapped out a whisper campaign to get the crowd buzzing, "Jesus is out to undermine the Justice Center by drawing attention to himself."

The officials at the kingdom Justice Center didn't need Lucifer to point out that Jesus was a threat. They watched Jesus closely, looking for an opportunity to discredit him and bring him down.

Offer of Kingdom Citizenship

The crowds were intrigued by the turf war, but they were really excited about the miracles. Jesus knew he needed to address the believability factor. He knew that a man claiming to represent the King of a superpower nation in another dimension needed to back up his words with a little proof.

For person after person, Jesus used his diplomatic authority over the dimensions of the universe to do things that are impossible for beings locked in three dimensions.

"I'm doing these miracles, these demonstrations of kingdom power, for two reasons," he explained to his honorary consuls, gathered around their evening campfire.

"Fame and fortune?" asked John, known by the group as one of the boisterous thunder brothers. John's brother, James, gave him a corrective slap on the back of his head.

"Thank you, James." Jesus smiled. "No, John, not even close," he continued. "First, it's to show that the kingdom of heaven has a huge desire and ability to meet the needs of its citizens. Receiving a miracle gives a taste of what it's like when one is released from the chains of these three dimensions."

"Secondly, I do them to show the crowds that the reality of the kingdom is far bigger than what they can detect with their senses and understand with their minds—that what they have always believed about the King and the kingdom is *really real*."

Jesus did many miracles in front of many eyewitnesses, feeding crowds of thousands from virtually nothing, turning hundreds of gallons of water into the same amount of fine wine, withering a tree by speaking to it—jaw-dropping miracles for sure—but the most impressive were the healings. Person after person came to Jesus and he cured them of lifelong incurable infirmities including blindness, paralysis, and mental illness. In most cases, however, Jesus told the person being healed not to tell anyone.

The capstone of his miracles was when Jesus' friend Lazarus died. Four days after his friend's death, Jesus stood in front of Lazarus' tomb with dozens watching. He called directly up to the top floor of heaven, "Father! King of heaven! I know that *you* know the plan, but I'm shouting this so everyone watching me here will know that this miracle is *your* doing!"

The King nodded, watching through the Crystal Sea portal. Jesus turned to the tomb and said, "Lazarus, come out!"

An attendant in the kingdom arrivals lounge tapped the new arrival on the shoulder, interrupting his conversation. He whispered, "Mr. Lazarus, please come with me right away."

Moments later, Lazarus found himself back in his body, staggering toward the open door of his tomb. Everyone was astounded, including Lazarus.

Word of the miracles, this one in particular, spread fast all over the country, and Jesus drew huge crowds, hundreds and even thousands at a time. Often, they showed up to see the miracles and totally missed the message. So when the people saw the miracles, Jesus would challenge them, "Even if you don't understand or believe what I'm saying, at *least* believe me because of the miracles you have seen with your own eyes!"[13]

As he traveled throughout Israel on his kingdom awareness tour, Jesus was constantly dogged by Justice Center staff members who had been sent by their superiors to pepper Jesus with trick questions, trying to trip him up in front of the people. They usually found that they were the ones to be embarrassed by Jesus' common sense, yet deeply profound answers.

After disposing of a trick question, Jesus would turn his back on the antagonists and remind the crowd of the

Offer of Kingdom Citizenship

dangers of being blindly committed to anyone or anything other than the kingdom and the Royals themselves.

The thing which really infuriated the men from the kingdom Justice Center was when, right in front of them, Jesus would look a person in the eye and say, "We both know that you have broken the prime directive of heaven, but I hereby grant you a full pardon from your death sentence under kingdom law."

The Justice Center staffers nearly had a stroke! "Now he's handing out pardons for kingdom violations! Who does this guy think he is, the Prince of heaven or something?"

Jesus had no patience for the Justice Center bureaucrats. "You wouldn't know a Royal if you were standing in front of one! You think handing out kingdom pardons is hard for me? You don't even know who I am! How hard do you think *this* is?" Jesus turned to a nearby crippled person and said, "Get up and walk!" Jesus then turned and glared at the bureaucrats, as the man jumped up off the floor, whooping and hopping.[14]

On the way out of town, Jesus and his entourage walked along a dusty highway. Peter and John had been talking about Jesus and those amazing healings. When they came alongside Jesus, Peter blurted, "Jesus, we're not trying to tell you what to do, but when you heal people like that, it's big news. If you just tell them who you really are—the Prince of the kingdom of heaven—word would get around. They're all guessing that you are the Prince, but you don't ever tell them! You even tell them not to say anything about the miracles.[15] I don't get it."

They walked in silence for another twenty paces and Jesus asked, "You're not trying to tell me what to do?"

"Oh, no, of course not," Peter responded immediately. John shook his head in agreement.

It was another twenty paces before Peter blurted, "But if I *was* telling you what to do, I'd say, 'Just tell them!'"

Jesus laughed as they kept walking.

Lucifer was not laughing. "This Prince is walking through my planet, inciting people to openly defy and reject me, their lawful ruler!"

If he could, Lucifer would have orchestrated an unfortunate accident to have Jesus killed. The trouble for Lucifer was that Jesus was no mere human, but a citizen of the kingdom. But there was more—back at the Jordan, the Prime Minister had given Jesus not only a kingdom passport, but full diplomatic credentials as well. Jesus' diplomatic credentials were that of a senior kingdom ambassador, giving access to resources in every dimension of the universe.

Lucifer, however, was locked into the lower frontier, just the dimensions of the earth and the heavenlies. "I can't even *see* those other dimensions any more," he said, knowing how much power could be wielded through them. Lucifer knew full well he was no match for Jesus. "Damn that Prince! I can't lay a hand on him directly," he thought in anger. "But I *have* to get him off my planet somehow. The boys over at the Justice Center are really mad at Jesus and *they* want him out of the picture as well. There's no telling what they might do if I just give them a little help."

The chief justice was livid. "This Jesus is telling the people to get right with the kingdom, but he isn't even pointing them to the kingdom Justice Center! Who does he think he is? He's rewriting the books of Israel's founding fathers! He announced that he can *personally* issue kingdom pardons! Only the Prince of heaven can do that! Jesus is a liar and a deceiver! This is *treason*!"

Other Justice Center officials saw which way the wind was blowing and piled on, "He publicly mocks the Justice

Offer of Kingdom Citizenship

Center and all of us, calling us walking dead men. He says *we* will be excluded from the kingdom's plan for Israel!"[16]

"Enough!" shouted the chief justice. "This man Jesus is an enemy of Israel and of heaven's prime directive. He has to die for the good of the nation!"

The PM turned to the Father and said, "The chief justice doesn't know how right he is!"

"If he did," the Father replied, "he might not go through with it."[17]

Jesus' kingdom citizenship awareness tour had been going on for almost three years. Before Jesus and his followers turned toward Jerusalem, Jesus had them set up camp at the base of a mountain. The next morning, Jesus called, "Peter! James! John! Come with me. I want to show you something. The rest of you stay here. We'll be back in a few hours."

Without a word, the four of them climbed the rocky slope, finally making it to the small, flat peak. They were dusting themselves off when Jesus seemed to light up as if he were glowing from within. The light became incredibly intense, and two other bright figures came from nowhere, and stood beside Jesus. Peter, James and John jumped back. They watched and listened as the three bright figures greeted each other and spoke of some mass exodus, which was just about to start—a migration of humans across the border from earth into the kingdom.[18]

Peter recognized the others, and whispered to John, "It's Moses and Elijah—founding fathers of Israel! They've crossed the border to meet us." He called out, "Jesus!"

The three glowing figures suddenly stopped their conversation and turned their heads in Peter's direction. "We need to make some monuments here—to you!" Peter shouted. "Everyone, everywhere will know who you really are and what you are going to do! We have to tell them!"

Moses whispered, "Is he trying to blow your cover?" Jesus shook his head slightly. "No," Jesus whispered back, "he just doesn't understand the plan."[19] All three quietly looked at Peter, who was beginning to think the monument thing wasn't such a good idea. Behind the bright figures, a dark cloud boiled up, quickly engulfing them. Moses immediately recognized what was happening. It was the Prince's father. Moses recognized the King from their meeting in the clouds on Mount Sinai. A voice boomed from within the cloud, directed at Peter, James and John, "This is my son! Listen to him!"[20]

As quickly as it began, the cloud receded. Moses and Elijah left with it, and the glow within Jesus faded. "C'mon, lets go," Jesus said to his friends. "Now listen this time—do *not* tell anyone who I really am!" Jesus headed down the steep slope, then paused and turned, "At least not until I return from the dead." The three men were baffled by the part about returning from the dead. They kept their mouths shut regardless.[21]

They rejoined their friends for dinner in camp. In the morning, they headed for Jerusalem.

Into the hornet's nest," Lucifer grinned. "All according to plan."

Completing the Transaction

The Prime Minister turned to the Royal Father. "All according to plan," he said somberly. The King nodded.

Jesus made a triumphant entry into Jerusalem amidst thousands of cheering admirers. Later that week, knowing he was about to die, Jesus organized a quiet dinner with his closest friends, so they could talk privately. He wanted them to be ready when, very soon, the border would be opened to anyone from earth with a kingdom passport.

Over dinner, he told his friends what was about to happen. "First, one of you is going to turn me in to the authorities."

Judas, one of the honorary consuls, suddenly realized that Jesus knew everything. Earlier, Judas had secretly gone to the Justice Center and had offered to help them forcibly arrest Jesus. He had hoped this would compel Jesus to, once and for all, use his kingdom authority to put the justices and the Romans in their place; however, at this moment, his plan didn't seem very smart at all, and he felt as stupid as Adam wearing a fig leaf.

Lucifer, who had been watching from a corner, said to himself, "No turning back now, Judas." He walked briskly across the room through an upper dimension and entered into Judas' human body.

No one in the room could see it happen except Jesus, who looked sternly into the eyes of Judas, addressing Lucifer, and said, "Just do it."[1]

As soon as Judas left the room, taking Lucifer with him, kingdom guards descended into the room like a SWAT team. All of Lucifer's henchmen were hustled away, well out of hearing range. It was clear that the Royals wanted to keep the rest of the dinner conversation in the family, at least for now.[2]

Before the end of dinner, Jesus told them he had kept the best for last. "You all know that at the Justice Center, the blood of innocent animals is offered up so the people's condemnation can be covered. But we all know there is that nagging dilemma. Your kingdom record is covered and five minutes after you leave the Justice Center, it happens. It's always something, isn't it? The animal's lifeblood is effective only on clearing *past* violations, but your whole life is lived in the present and in the future. You are in violation again, usually before you get home!"

All the consuls had thought about that very question, but even thinking about it too much gave one a headache.

Jesus explained, "Since Adam left the garden, all humans have been prisoners in the dimension of time. You are continuously being dragged through time in only one direction—forward. The lifeblood of the animal covers your kingdom violations up until the time of its death, not beyond, because the animals are being dragged through time just like you. You cannot go back and use that death to cover violations in the future."

He paused to let his words sink in. "What you need is an innocent, willing, *human* substitute with *pure Royal blood*, who is not a prisoner of time, whose life isn't measured in the drip, drip, drip of one hour after another

Completing the Transaction

until he dies. For his sacrifice to be valid for all time, past, present, and future, your substitute needs to be present in *all of time at once*."

No one said anything. Peter, the first honorary consul chosen by Jesus, broke the silence. "That's what we need?" he asked, clearly confused.

"That's what you need," said Jesus, knowing his words were hard to grasp. Jesus continued, "And get this—*I am from above*—above the dimensions of earth, above length, width, height, time and above the heavenlies.[3] I am the innocent, willing, human substitute with pure Royal blood that will cover your kingdom violations *forever*. The old kingdom Justice Center is going out of business and *I* am replacing it.[4]

"Let me say that again: I will *personally* be the new kingdom Justice Center, so anyone who wants to have their kingdom record cleared once and forever must come to me, and I will clear it *if* they ask me to."

The men nodded slowly, knowing this was incredibly important, but very unsure of exactly what Jesus was saying. He put it in plain language for them.

"By this time tomorrow, I will be put to death by those who run the kingdom Justice Center. They will have the help and support of the Romans who run the rest of the world. But don't let anyone ever tell you that 'this person or that group of people *murdered* Jesus.'[5] This is *my* choice. I am doing this willingly as part of the kingdom plan to buy back the earth and the humans who inhabit it. *I am the One*, the *willing*, qualified substitute, who was first promised four thousand years ago in the garden.

"So, everything you have heard about how to clear your kingdom record with the lifeblood of animals is true and consistent, from Adam and Eve until now. From this point forward, I am your substitute; I am above time, so the value of my death for you is once and for always, covering past, present, and future. From now on, anyone who renounces their earthly citizenship and claims *me* as their substitute will be eligible for kingdom citizenship. The Prime Minister will issue kingdom passports to all who become citizens, and those with kingdom passports can *never* be turned away at the kingdom gates.[6]

"Best of all," Jesus added with a smile, "the kingdom is in dimensions above time. When you enter the kingdom, you enter dimensions above time as well. In the kingdom, time never runs out and we all live forever.

"When you know for certain that you are a citizen of the kingdom and that you will live forever, even after your body is gone, it's *very* freeing," Jesus said. "You can leave behind any constant worrying about the minutia of kingdom law, or even the ups and downs of life. You are free to focus on the big picture of building the kingdom with me."[7]

Knowing that they were only catching a small percentage of what he was telling them, Jesus continued. The PM would help them make sense of it later.

"In a few days I will come with the Prime Minister and bring your kingdom passports. After I have left the earth and returned across the border into the kingdom, the Prime Minister will again visit each of you to deliver diplomatic credentials establishing your status as ambassadors of the kingdom, and confirming the trusted relationship you have with the Royals."[8]

"As ambassadors, do not hesitate to call in the kingdom military as needed. The Prime Minister will provide you with weaponry effective in all dimensions, not just the three dimensions of earth.[9] You *will* need them since the enemies of the kingdom live in dimensions outside of plain sight.[10] Don't worry," the Prince told them. "I personally have overcome everything he's got to throw at you, and I will be with you always."[11]

Completing the Transaction

Jesus looked around the room at his team of honorary consuls, who were stone silent. They were just now realizing that, while they may become ambassadors, it was apparent that they were about to be posted in a war zone.

"Oh, and this is really important," Jesus said. "If anyone asks you to help them become a kingdom citizen, all of you are authorized to accept their renunciation of the warlord and their commitment to me. The Prime Minister will be with you and he can issue regular kingdom passports, on the spot, guaranteeing the new citizen's entry into the kingdom."

"If anyone who is already a kingdom citizen tells you they want to be a kingdom ambassador and get into the fight, you can bring them to the Prime Minister. He will make the call on exactly what they need and how they should be used in the Diplomatic Corps."

They all nodded. Jesus knew that for them, a full understanding would come, but not tonight. "Don't worry that you don't understand everything," Jesus told them. "The Prime Minister will help you remember everything I have said to you."[12]

Toward the end of the evening, Jesus again asked for their attention. "For centuries, the innocent blood of animals from your household has been poured out for you, over and over at the kingdom Justice Center." Jesus lifted a cup of wine from the table and looked at it. After a pause, he said, "The wine in this cup is my Royal blood. Soon, my blood will be poured out and kingdom justice will be satisfied for everyone who claims me as their substitute. In Egypt, Israel painted their doors with the blood of the lamb. Paint your hearts with mine." He took a sip and passed the cup around the table.

He then picked up a loaf of bread and said to his honorary consuls, "The death of my body tomorrow is what will sustain all of you in this world, just like the manna dropped by the kingdom sustained your ancestors in the wilderness. Here," he said as he took some and passed the loaf around, "break off a piece and eat it. Remember that my body is broken for you, and my death will be what sustains you all the way through passport control in the kingdom."[13]

They spoke until late in the evening. The honorary consuls felt like they had been hit with a fire hose of last minute information. It was way too much to take in all at once.

"Let's go," said the Prince.

Together they went out past the kingdom security team standing guard and through the east gate of Jerusalem and waited in a garden, in the dark of night.

Seeing them coming, Lucifer said, "It's show time!"

The next twelve hours were a cacophony of confrontation, arrest, and accusations, with all the noise coming from the accusers. "I want to hear you say it! Are you the Prince of the Kingdom, the One promised in the Garden four thousand years ago?" Jesus hardly spoke, and when he did, it only infuriated the accusers.[14] Jesus endured verbal abuse as well as brutal and bloody physical assaults. The Roman governor, Pilate, asked Jesus directly if he, Jesus, was actually a king. "Yes," Jesus answered, "but my kingdom is not of this world."[15]

"Enough with the nonsensical answers! Don't you know that I have the power to put you to death right now?" demanded Pilate.

Jesus, dripping blood on the marble floor of Pilate's foyer, said softly, "You wouldn't have any power at all if my Father hadn't given it to you."[16]

Not knowing what to do with an answer like that from a man who should have been very intimidated, and facing an unruly mob of locals calling for Jesus' death, Pilate did a quick calculation. He then did the politically expedient thing; Jesus was flogged, taken outside the city, and was nailed to a cross, the preferred method of execution in the Roman Empire.[17]

Along with two other condemned men, the Prince of heaven hung in public view to die a slow-motion death. It was a surreal view from the perspective of the men on the cross. People gawked at them from just a few feet away, some in stunned silence, some chatting and milling about. Some were just doing their jobs, making sure the execution went off without any trouble.[18]

The condemned man on his left side turned his head and insulted Jesus with his final breaths, "You phony. If you really are the Prince, how could you let this happen?"

"Shut up," gasped the dying man on Jesus' right. "We deserve to die. He doesn't. Prince," he gasped, "remember me—when you get home to your kingdom."

Jesus gathered what was left of his strength and replied, "You will be with me at the kingdom gates today."[19]

As the Prince breathed his final breaths as a human, he felt the entire, fearsome weight of the kingdom's legal system crushing down on him. He was personally absorbing the rightful punishment due all who flaunt the kingdom's prime directive: *Total allegiance to the King.*

The Prince cried out to his father, but kingdom communications were cut off and the border was shut tight. Jesus was under condemnation, and heaven was sealed off. He hung there in agony and finally died, alone.[20]

The normally bustling great kingdom hall was totally silent. The Royal Father was on his throne, eyes closed, and his head tilted back. The Prime Minister sat nearby, leaning forward, his head buried in his hands.

On earth, just out of human sight, Lucifer was high-fiving every one of his soldiers surrounding him. This was a time to celebrate! The invader had been turned back! The human Prince was dead—put to death by the humans he came to save!

"And when those Royals try to claim that Jesus was the acceptable substitute—here to save the humans from kingdom law—*Wham!*" Lucifer slapped his hand on his thigh, "Got him! Jesus, Crusher, The One, what-*ever* your name is! You are from *my* bloodline, *my* household, *my* earth! You can pick up your marbles and go home, Prince. Get off my earth, *NOW!*"

When Jesus breathed his last, there was first a ripple, followed by tremors on the earth, then a violent shaking.

Lucifer and his followers stood in stunned silence and watched. At the Royal Father's command, over one thousand members of the kingdom Corps of Engineers grabbed the fabric of the universe, the curtains dividing the dimensions, and began to twist them. First they warped, then they stretched, and finally, a hole was torn.[21] They had torn a permanent wormhole in the universe from the dimensions of heaven to the dimensions of earth.

While there had been temporary wormholes before, this new one was the first permanent road between the three dimensions of earth and the highest dimensions of the heavens. Kingdom engineers were already busy setting up a border crossing checkpoint to allow access for kingdom citizens. The road was not very wide, however. It was actually quite narrow, and its entrance on the earth's end was in the heavenlies, just out of sight for the humans. By design, a human on earth couldn't find it at all unless the Prime Minister or one of the ambassadors would lead them to it.[22]

Lucifer, however, could see the new border crossing. "What does he think he is doing? Nobody is going up that road! Jesus is not *qualified* as a kingdom-substitute because he is part of *my* household, *my* bloodline and I *forbid* it! He is *not* an acceptable substitute under kingdom law!"

Completing the Transaction

He shook his fist upwards, shouting "If you let these people up that road into the kingdom, I am coming up too and so are all my troops! If you don't let us in, our whole deal is off!"

Outwardly defiant, but trembling inside, the warlord of the earth waited silently for a reply. He didn't have to wait long.

Lucifer's lieutenant ran breathless to his leader, "They have tricked us! It's pure Royal blood!"

"What is this nonsense?" he demanded. "Make sense!"

"I overheard some kingdom soldiers. They were *laughing* at us![23] They were saying that the bloodline in this Jesus is 100% pure Royal blood."

"Impossible! All of you were encouraging the women and men of Israel, and the rest of the world for that matter, to sleep with whomever they wanted—and I know they were doing it. After all these centuries, that so called Royal bloodline is now mine, and I can prove it!" he screamed.

"I'm telling you, Jesus is *totally* of the Royal bloodline," Lucifer's lieutenant continued. "The girl, his mother, was a *virgin*. No man had ever touched her. They said the Prime Minister of heaven is the baby's father."

"*I* knew she was a virgin!" Lucifer protested. "I read what those founding fathers had written about that. So what? Virgin or not, she is part of *my* bloodline. After Rahab and all the others, I own the stinking human bloodline!"

"You are completely right about that, sir. You have done a masterful job in capturing Israel's bloodline. However," he continued, "it seems that when the Prince created humans, he constructed them so that no blood from the mother ever comes in contact with the baby—not ever.[24] Blood doesn't even exist in a baby until the father's contribution starts the process. His bloodline is 100% pure Royal, because the Prime Minister of heaven is the father.

The Royals have taken an end run around our claim to his bloodline. It'll be hard to convince any judge that Jesus isn't an acceptable substitute—not on the basis of his bloodline anyway."

Lucifer stood in stunned silence, staring at nothing.

Fearing the traditional shooting of the messenger, Lucifer's lieutenant made a silent and hasty exit as Lucifer processed the devastating news.

Border Opens for Kingdom Citizens

The Prince was released from his human body of thirty-three years, which the rulers of earth had turned into a torture chamber. He was lifted out of the dead body of Jesus by a kingdom military honor guard and brought to the kingdom citizens' arrival lounge.[1]

As the Prince rested in the lounge, he turned to the man on his right who had also just arrived. Jesus smiled and said, "I told you we'd both be here together today." All the man who had been on the cross next to Jesus could say was, "Thank you, Prince! Thank you!"

The Prince got up to greet his friends[2] in the lounge and announced, "This has been a big day and it's not over yet." With that, he walked out of the lounge and headed down the concourse, through the security gate, down a long corridor, past the entrance to the lower waiting room. The lighting became very dim. The heat was stifling. At the end of the hallway was a heavy metal door. Etched in stone above the door was a single word:

TARTARUS

The door was guarded by a kingdom trooper. He dropped to one knee as the Prince approached. The Prince nodded and the guard rose to open the door. As he pulled, the hinges creaked and, like breaking the seal on a jar, air rushed through the crack as it opened.

Inside, hundreds, maybe thousands, of Lucifer's troops squatted in the darkness, murmuring.[3] They immediately fell silent and all locked eyes on the Prince. Most of them had been locked in the darkness since shortly after leaving the heavenlies behind, to pursue the human women of earth, thousands of years earlier. Realizing this was not a rescue by their general, they all fell to their knees.[4]

"If you haven't heard," the Prince said in a loud steady voice, "the war is over. Hostilities may continue for a while, but your General Lucifer has lost." The murmuring grew and quickly faded as they leaned forward for more news. "All humans, regardless of their ancestry, can once again become part of the Royal bloodline of heaven and regain their kingdom citizenship."

He paused to let the news sink in. "You gave up everything to become like men, and so you will be judged like men. As I promised when you were deported from the kingdom, each of you will face trial, but I will not judge you. The humans whom you violated will be your judges."[5]

The Prince looked deeply into the eyes of the warriors who, before the General's rebellion, had served bravely in his kingdom army. He sighed, and silently exited the dungeon. The door slammed shut behind him as he strode purposefully up the corridor towards earth.

Jesus died on Friday. At daybreak on Sunday, the Prince returned to the earth in a strong, new human body. It looked much like the old one, even bearing the same scars.

At the Prince's command, one of the kingdom soldiers rolled the stone away from the entrance to the tomb. The Roman soldiers who had been posted to prevent grave tampering sat on the ground, unable to stand, and watched. They were as motionless as they were speechless. A few moments later, they both got up and bolted in the direction of the Jerusalem city gate.

The Prince walked out of the tomb. He was almost out of the garden when he heard a voice calling from behind him, but not calling him by name.

"Where is he?" she called. He knew that voice well. It was Mary, one of his most loyal friends.

Mary was unaware that the man she was speaking to was Jesus until he turned and said, "Mary!" She was stunned. He was supposed to be dead!

She ran toward him, arms ready for a hug, saying, "Jesus!"

The Prince had a huge smile and held up his hands to discourage the hug. "Whoa, Mary. Stop! You cannot touch me until after I see my father. I need to go to the throne room before anyone touches me, but I'll be right back.[6] Go tell my honorary consuls that you've seen me this morning."

Jesus vanished from Mary's sight when he turned onto the kingdom highway, through the newly opened wormhole. The gates swung open and he was greeted with the thunderous cheering of thousands who lined both sides of the road. He strode purposefully toward the throne room.[7]

Before Mary had gone all the way back to the room where the honorary consuls were staying, Jesus had finished his most important meeting with his father. Jesus met her again on the path, and this time he didn't flinch, letting her give him a big hug.[8]

5: Transition of Power
Local Resistance

As promised, Jesus returned to the earth in his new body, designed for easy movement through the dimensions of earth, as well as through all the other dimensions of the universe.[1]

In his new body, the Prince traveled through Israel for forty days, but not always in the conventional way. He used a number of higher-dimensional shortcuts to get where he was going. Time after time, Jesus would suddenly, apparently out of nowhere, step into the presence of people in locked rooms or in private conversations. After engaging them for a while, the Prince would leave, not by walking out the door, but by simply vanishing from their sight.[2] While astonishing to them, from Jesus' new perspective, he was simply stepping out of the room.

When Jesus did step in or out of the earthly dimensions like that, he usually gave people a jolt, even those who knew him well. He would suddenly appear, and they would act like he was a ghost. "Don't be afraid," Jesus would say. "Look at me, touch me. I've got skin and bones just like you. I'm no ghost! Give me something to eat and I'll prove it."[3] Eventually, they would calm down and listen to him.

In his first such meeting, the Prime Minister joined the Prince. Jesus told the honorary consuls, "Congratulations men! Because I have cleared your kingdom record once and for always, and because you have publicly committed yourselves to me and to my kingdom, you are now full citizens of the kingdom of heaven. Receive your kingdom passports!"[4]

Standing directly in front of the group in an unseen upper dimension, the Prime Minister went from man to man and reached his hand into each chest, sliding in their new kingdom passports as if into a pocket.[5] He looked at them proudly, then stepped up and out of the room, returning to the kingdom proper.

The Prince continued, "All the rights, privileges, and responsibilities of citizenship in the kingdom of heaven are now yours. And by the way, you are no longer honorary consuls. As citizens of heaven, you are now consuls of the kingdom, no longer just honorary."

"And that means … ?" asked Peter.

Jesus replied, "It means you are still official representatives of the kingdom, commissioned by the Prime Minister, but now you do it as citizens, kingdom *insiders*. Your job is the same—bring as many humans as possible through the citizenship process. Help everyone who wants to immigrate to heaven."

"But for you," Jesus added, "there will be more. You will be the first ambassadors to the earth from the kingdom of heaven.

As ambassadors, will have an open line to the Prime Minister, and he will provide you with access to the kingdom arsenal. Trust me, you will *need* these weapons when the enemy comes out of the heavenlies against you.[6] Whenever you call on me, know that the Prime Minister

Local Resistance

will support you with the full power and authority of the kingdom."

Peter asked, "But all that authority—how will we even know how to use it? You *know* we have failed miserably at even the simple things you have taught us."

Jesus smiled and put his hand on his friend's shoulder, "I will head back across the border soon, and I will send the Prime Minister. He will make it clear exactly what your tasks are." Jesus added, "You never saw me do *anything* that the King didn't tell me to do. The Prime Minister will keep you on track with kingdom policies and initiatives. The only thing is that you've got to *listen* to him and *trust* what he tells you. And, be bold enough to act on it! Got it?"

They nodded.

"But don't go anywhere yet," Jesus warned.[7] "As the kingdom Diplomatic Corps, you have all been targeted by the enemy—you are marked men." Jesus looked at the fearsome kingdom military guards one dimension above, surrounding their little group. "You are safe right here until the Prime Minister brings your diplomatic credentials and a secure communications link is established with the kingdom. Once all the security measures are in place, the Prime Minister will provide your global deployment instructions."[8]

It was time for the Prince to leave earth and return to the kingdom. He met with his consuls and other close friends on a hillside in Galilee to make a stunning geopolitical announcement: "Lucifer's reign on this planet is officially over. I have fulfilled everything required to reclaim the earth for the kingdom. Effective immediately, I have been given all legal authority over both the kingdom and the earth."[9]

The diplomats glanced at each other, wondering what this world-changing news would mean.

"Lucifer is refusing to relinquish his grip on the earth and its people—he will fight us to the death—but he cannot hold back the forward march of the kingdom. Rest assured that he will be removed.[10] He is only allowed to remain for a time because you have a job to do first. As kingdom diplomats, you need to tell everyone, everywhere, that Lucifer is finished. He and anyone who remains loyal to him will *not* be allowed to stay in the kingdom when its borders are officially moved around the earth."[11]

"Tell the people," Jesus said with a calm urgency, "tell *all* of them.[12] If they want to even *see* the kingdom, they *must* become kingdom citizens. Tell them citizenship is free. They just need to apply for it."[13]

With that, Jesus, the Prince of heaven, said farewell to his friends. "You may not see me, but trust me—I will be with you." He turned slowly up the narrow, newly paved kingdom highway, through the border crossing, and into the throne room of his father.

The Prince was greeted by a crowd of millions. Every being in the kingdom had turned out for the triumphant return of the Prince. He took his seat next to his very proud father while the Prime Minister made preparations for his own imminent departure.

The soon-to-be-ambassadors were very excited. It was a nervous excitement that stayed with them as they settled back into Jerusalem to wait as they had been told. Waiting is hard when you know the entire world, including your own life, is about to be turned upside down.

They stayed close together. Nobody wanted to miss a thing. The kingdom guard continued to keep watch as Lucifer and his men paced nervously.

The Prime Minister, the Prince and the King walked with Michael and Gabriel along the new kingdom highway toward the earth. They paused just short of the border crossing on the kingdom side.

Local Resistance

"You know there will be a lot of hate directed at our citizens, because of the Prince," Michael said to the Prime Minister.

"No kidding," replied the PM with mock surprise. "Humans are renouncing their citizenship on earth and are turning their backs on its ruler because of the Prince. No wonder the earth's establishment hates them. It hates us too, you know."[14]

"It doesn't matter what our enemies feel about us, Michael," the Prince added. "The Prime Minister will give them everything they need to protect themselves.[15] I told them they would receive direct orders to go out into every place on earth, to tell everyone about immigration to the kingdom. I wouldn't send them out unless they were fully armed, right PM?"

"I will see to it that my ambassadors will be able to exercise the full power and authority of the kingdom," assured the Prime Minister. "They will have a direct line to the Royal family."

The King underscored the point, "These new ambassadors, and those under their protection, will have more firepower available to them than Lucifer ever saw when he was here in the kingdom. These will be the most well armed diplomats the earth has ever seen. As long as the ambassadors are coordinated with the Prime Minister, Lucifer has no chance against them. The only problem is if they let themselves get distracted with the stuff of life on earth."[16]

"What about the new citizens who don't aspire to become kingdom diplomats?" Gabriel asked.

"They are every bit as much a part of my kingdom as the ambassadors are," the King said with certainty. "But if an unarmed kingdom citizen gets caught in the crossfire with the enemy, well, they may get pushed around a bit."

"Pushed around, but never pushed out of the kingdom," the Prime Minister added.[17] "Better they should aspire to join our Diplomatic Corps, though."

"Absolutely," said the Prince.

All five stood at the border, looking out towards the earth.

"Take care of my family," the Prince said quietly to the Prime Minister.

"Hey, they're my family too!" the PM whispered back with a wink.

The King said, "Let the Prime Minister go, so he can do his job."

The three Royals embraced. The Prime Minister gave a nod to the generals and walked through the border into the heart of Jerusalem.

Lucifer paced back and forth in his mountain hideaway just south and one dimension up from Jerusalem.

"So kingdom justice has been satisfied forever. Anyone who wants, can have their kingdom record wiped clean permanently. It's a pardon from the King that makes them eligible for kingdom citizenship. Hmmm," Lucifer was mulling over the current situation.

It was taking him some time to process this, but Lucifer realized that the one thing he had counted on for thousands of years had slipped away. Lucifer had focused on capturing the bloodline to invalidate Crusher's qualifications to be the One, but the Royals did an end run. Jesus paid the ransom demanded by the mortgage and now kingdom pardons were freely available to humans. They could now become citizens of the kingdom!

"But what if I can get them to reject the pardon?" he pondered. "The King of heaven won't force anyone into taking it, not if these humans really have free will."[18] The more he thought about it, the more he liked the idea. He turned to his lieutenants and tested some lines for their next big whisper campaign.

"Kingdom pardon? No thanks. Where is the personal responsibility in someone else taking the blame?"

He tried another, "Accepting that pardon is like admitting you are a failure and you need someone's charity."

One of his officers chimed in, "Who needs a pardon anyway? Look at all the good things you've done. They *must* count for something!"

Another added, "Forget the pardon, you don't want to be lumped in with a bunch of people who have done despicable things and then beg for a pardon at the last minute. What was that King thinking anyway?"

Still another said, "Taking the pardon is the same as admitting you've done really, really bad things—but you are *not that bad*. In fact, you're pretty good. This pardon is for losers who haven't accomplished anything in life! It's a crutch for the weak! And *you* are strong!"

Lucifer offered his favorite, "You think God wants you, after the way you have let him down? Its embarrassing that you would even ask God for a pardon!"

He smiled, "We can work with this. Who would even *want* to ask for a kingdom pardon?"

It was a beautiful morning in Jerusalem, but all of the kingdom consuls were indoors. They were together in a large room inside the city walls, passing time in conversation, waiting as the Prince had told them.

They were not alone. Also in the room were a number of Jerusalem locals and foreigners from around the world, including Cyprus, Libya, Egypt, and Rome, to name a few.

The morning stillness was shattered as the Prime Minister entered the room through a wormhole from an unseen upper dimension. Everyone in the room heard the sound of a powerful gust of wind, which shook the house.[19]

The Prime Minister came to all of the consuls at once with the same flickering flame appearance that Moses saw on the bush in the desert more than a thousand years earlier. Everyone in the room saw it dancing on each of the consuls.

The Prime Minister reached into each consul's body and deposited their diplomatic credentials. To each he whispered, "You are now an ambassador of the kingdom of heaven!"

The new ambassadors jumped up, eyes wide and mouths open, when they realized what was happening. They started shouting at each other, but they didn't even recognize what they themselves were saying. They were all speaking different languages. "What is going on?" several onlookers wondered aloud.

The foreign bystanders realized before anyone else that these ambassadors were speaking in several foreign languages, *their own* languages! They were shouting an incredible message: "The borders of the kingdom of heaven are opening for immigration!"

"Comm links all check out sir," reported the senior communications officer in heaven. "All human languages plus the kingdom code are available and operational."

The Prince nodded in approval. He had included the kingdom code as part of the ambassador's equipment, since he was not about to let Lucifer listen-in on critical communications traffic with his ambassadors.[20]

Everyone was amazed. No one had ever heard of anything like this. The room was filled with the sound of voices, those of the ambassadors as well as those of the astonished onlookers.

The Prime Minister tapped ambassador Peter on the shoulder and whispered to him. Peter then stepped up, raised his hands and called for quiet in the room.

Local Resistance

"Some of you said you think we've been drinking," Peter said to the crowd. "You're wrong. It's much too early in the day for that!" A few in the crowd chuckled.

"Do you remember Jesus?" Peter asked loudly of the crowd.

Jesus had done countless miracles in Jerusalem over the past few years.[21] Yes, everybody here knew who Jesus was.

"Let me tell you who Jesus really is," Peter said. "Jesus is the Prince of the Royal family of the kingdom of heaven, the same Royal family who established our country Israel and protected it and provided for it since the beginning. Yes, I am saying he has lived forever! That's what people do in the kingdom of heaven—they live forever!

"Jesus came to offer each and every one of you that same eternal life. The kingdom is right here, in dimensions you cannot see with your eyes, above and beyond time." Peter shouted with a boldness no one had ever seen in him before, "Anybody want to be a citizen of the kingdom, and live forever?"

The crowd roared, "Yes!"

"Stand up and be counted as people who have turned their backs on the ruler of the earth. Publicly renounce him and all he stands for. Receive the full pardon that the kingdom offers you! Then publicly commit yourself and your family to the kingdom, and you will be received as kingdom citizens. The Prime Minister will issue you a kingdom passport. *That* will give you guaranteed passage through the border into heaven. Even when you die, you will live forever!"[22]

That day, three thousand people in Jerusalem renounced their citizenship of earth. With the help of the ambassadors, they applied for kingdom passports.

The word spread quickly and the staff at the kingdom Department of Immigration was busier than ever—and they were loving it.

The ambassadors were on a roll. The more people who accepted this offer to become kingdom citizens, the more people they told.

The ambassadors knew that the best place to spread the Prince's good news had to be at the kingdom Justice Center. After all, Jesus had told them, "I *am* the new kingdom Justice Center."

"Our citizenship is in heaven!" these ambassadors would shout on the way to the Justice Center.[23] "Turn your back on the ruler of earth and join us!"

The Roman soldiers who heard the ambassadors' message were not sure what to make of it. The ambassadors had said nothing about Rome or Caesar, or even Israel. It was as strange to the soldiers as it was amusing.

It was neither strange nor amusing to Lucifer. He knew exactly what was happening. The Prince had punched a hole in the border and if Lucifer didn't take some action, now, his entire human race would be rushing out of his lower frontier—out of his sphere of influence.

"I will not let this situation spin out of control," he said to himself. Lucifer strode toward the Justice Center. "The chief justice should be looking for some viable options just about now."

The judiciary at the kingdom Justice Center was indeed looking for options. They were getting close to full-scale panic. They looked out the window of their executive conference room to see those motley followers of Jesus, as they called them, at the front of a huge crowd right below their window. These unsophisticated men, these self-proclaimed kingdom ambassadors, were telling the crowds that people could be pardoned for violations of the kingdom's prime directive, without submitting to the authority of the Justice Center.

Caiaphas, the chief justice, understood at least some of what was happening. "The institution of the Justice Center is under attack. For over a thousand years, this has been the one and only place where people could come to escape the consequences of violating the kingdom's prime directive!"

"The Prince of heaven would be appalled," Lucifer whispered in the chief justice's ear. "He *personally* organized the first Justice Center. These traitors are feeding lies to the people."

Caiaphas turned to his associates and said calmly, "Our people have forgotten what it means to be a kingdom people. The Prince of heaven showed Moses and Aaron long ago the way to escape the death penalty at the Justice Center. These 'Jesus people' are offering a shortcut to justice where there is none. Our people are believing lies. It is our job to expose the liars."

"Look!" interrupted Nicodemus, pointing out the conference room window. The other justices gathered close around him. "It's that lame fellow who panhandles outside the main gate of the Justice Center. I know he can't walk, but there he is, prancing around like a fool." They saw Peter and John standing near the center of the crowd, just as much the center of attention as the former cripple.[24]

"Now *they* are doing it too!" Nicodemus exclaimed.

His associates knew Nicodemus was referring to the many healings, and even the raising of people from the dead, for which Jesus had become known. The chief justice knew that Nicodemus had spent quite a bit of time with Jesus before his execution, and he wasn't very sure about Nicodemus' political loyalties.

"Nicodemus," said the chief justice, "there is a *huge* difference between following the ancient teachings of the Prince of heaven as Israel has done for thousands of years, and following a man who *claimed* to be the Prince himself, but was then killed at the hands of mortal men. Can't you see how ridiculous and impossible that is? The eternal Prince of the kingdom being killed by mere men?"[25]

They could all hear the crowd below shouting, "Prince Jesus!"

"This is not the work of the Prince," whispered Lucifer smoothly. "These men are simply calling attention to themselves, distracting the people from true kingdom justice and the Justice Center."

"It's a trick." Caiaphas said quietly. "As I said, we simply need to expose the liars. Bring those friends of Jesus in so we can talk with them."

A security team from the Justice Center elbowed its way though the crowd. They grabbed John and Peter who were in the midst of telling the people how to apply for kingdom citizenship. They were dragged away, but before the crowd dispersed that evening, another two thousand applications had been processed and passports had been issued by the kingdom Department of Immigration.[26]

Peter and John spent the night in jail.[27] The next morning, they, along with a man they had healed, were brought before the chief justice and members of his judicial staff. Caiaphas had only one question, "By whose authority are you doing this?"

Peter, once a lowly fisherman from Galilee, now an ambassador of the superpower kingdom of the universe, looked the chief justice in the eye and said, "If you are asking about how we healed this man who could not walk yesterday, then I want to be very clear. We are ambassadors of the kingdom of heaven. It is by the power of the kingdom and the authority of the Prince of heaven that this man stands before you tall and healthy."

"Jesus from Nazareth, the One who you brought to Pilate to be killed, is that Prince of heaven. The King of heaven raised him back to life. Jesus, who you opposed, has become the new Justice Center. No one can have their record permanently cleared, and get kingdom citizenship, unless they accept a kingdom pardon from Jesus."[28]

Local Resistance

The justices were speechless. Caiaphas ordered the guards to remove the three men from the room. Once they were alone, they discussed their options.

"What are we going to do with these men? They know *nothing* about kingdom law, but they claim to have a new Justice Center! What nonsense!"

"But that *was* an outstanding miracle. Everyone saw it and we can't deny it."

"We cannot let them keep stirring up the people like this," said Caiaphas. "Just think about it. The real Prince of Heaven wouldn't keep changing the law. He wouldn't build our Justice Center, and then suddenly abandon it. We may not understand all of this, but we do know that these men are seducing our people away from the Justice Center that the true Prince of heaven established himself—and that is just wrong! Bring the prisoners back in!"

The chief justice gave the men a tongue lashing, reminded them of two thousand years of national history and tradition, and ordered them to stop their divisive behavior immediately.[29]

Peter and John listened respectfully. When it was their turn to respond, Peter said, "Ask yourself what you would do in my place. Obey a man from earth, or obey the King of the universe? We cannot keep quiet about this."

"That doesn't sound much like Peter the fisherman," the King remarked to his son as they watched events unfold from the throne room.

"Amazing! PM certainly is inspiring our ambassadors," said the Prince. "Just look at that!" They watched as Peter and John arrived at the home of a new kingdom citizen who was hosting an Independence Day party with the ambassadors and a number of new citizens. They celebrated their new citizenship and the opening of the kingdom borders by singing patriotic songs of the kingdom, with speeches and rounds of cheering for the Prince.

"PM has the ball and he is certainly running with it!" smiled the Prince, as his father nodded in agreement.[30]

Citizenship Application Deadline
ও৵

The Prime Minister had his ambassadors fired up. They could not think about anything other than getting the word out about the kingdom. While the Prince often spoke to the crowds with stories that were admittedly cryptic, the ambassadors were all about straight talk. They met with people every day in Jerusalem, reminding them about what Jesus had said, and answering questions about the kingdom.

The ambassadors' number one priority was always the same, to make sure that as many people as possible would hear that the kingdom was opening its borders to those with kingdom passports.

Anywhere they had the opportunity, the ambassadors promoted the kingdom. They were even brazen enough to hold a major citizenship drive at the Jerusalem Justice Center again.[1]

"This is outrageous!" Chief Justice Caiaphas shouted. "They are continuing to make a mockery of the Justice Center! Bring them up here now!" The security chief ran out with his men to grab the troublemakers.

Caiaphas was furious. Sharp words and accusations were thrown and fired back.

"Don't back down!" the Prime Minister whispered to Peter. "Speak the truth! The Prince and I will be your shield and your sword!"

"Don't back down!" Lucifer whispered into the chief justice's ear. "Speak the truth! Everyone knows you speak for the Prince of heaven. These men are traitors!"

"The battle for hearts and minds enters a new phase," the King said to his son.

"Lucifer is frantic to hold onto as many humans as he possibly can," responded the Prince. "But our ambassadors and the PM are hustling to get as many passports issued as possible."

In Jerusalem, Caiaphas signed an executive order authorizing his political officers to seek out and discipline revolutionaries. A revolutionary was anyone who attacked their traditional values with the destructive notion that this dead man Jesus was a replacement for the Justice Center in Jerusalem.

One of the most notorious enforcers of the Justice Center was an ambitious and well-schooled young man named Saul, who had made a name for himself as an up-and-comer in the Justice Center hierarchy. He had even participated in the first stoning execution of one of the revolutionaries. Caiaphas had no question about Saul's loyalty. He authorized Saul to use any means necessary to capture and bring these rebels back to Jerusalem to face the consequences of their treason against Israel.

"Now there's a man of action," the Prince said to his father. "Action and passion. Off-track for sure, but this guy has the potential to be a one-man kingdom Diplomatic Corps."

"He's also a Roman citizen, so he can cross any border on earth to get the word out about your kingdom and enroll citizens," replied the King. "Go introduce yourself to him,

Citizenship Application Deadline

son. It's time for Saul to begin a new life—to be born into our kingdom!"

The Prince headed down to earth to intercept Saul, who was on his way to break up a kingdom citizenship rally in Damascus. The Prince stood in the middle of the road, just out of human sight in the heavenlies. Saul rounded the bend with his entourage. As Saul passed just inches away, the Prince reached into the three dimensions of earth and grabbed him, yanking Saul to the ground, and pulling him partially into the heavenlies. Saul was blinded by the brilliant light coming from the Prince's face in this higher dimension. Saul's comrades could see he was frightened. They couldn't see the Prince at all—but they heard everything.

"Saul!" yelled the Prince, inches from his face. "What are you *doing*?"

"Who *are* you?" Saul implored, now fully blinded.

The Prince explained. "I am Jesus, the Prince of the kingdom, son of the King of heaven. You, Saul, are terrorizing citizens of my kingdom and that is going to stop right now!"

Having Saul's full attention, Jesus told him where to go and what to do to get his vision back. Saul was more than ready to comply.[2]

As Saul recovered he was visited by the Prime Minister who taught him everything he needed to know about the kingdom. In time, the former "muscle" of the Justice Center became a kingdom citizen, and even the most prominent ambassador of the kingdom. The PM issued his passport and diplomatic credentials. Like Abram two thousand years earlier, the Prince "made a name for him." From now on, Saul would be known throughout the earth as Paul.

Ultimately, Paul become as headstrong an ambassador of the kingdom as he had been as a Justice Center enforcer, but this time he had the full power and authority of the kingdom and its armed forces to back him up.

"The environment is just too hostile to open a kingdom consulate here," Paul told the new citizens as they gathered in the locked home of one of his friends in Jerusalem. "For now we will continue to meet together in secret, but you need to continue to invite those who want to defect to the kingdom."

"We'll never get the word out if we stay underground," said one of the enthusiastic new citizens.

"Everything in its time," responded Paul. "The Prime Minister has directed that I start establishing kingdom consulates throughout the Mediterranean region. I'm heading out shortly to do just that."

Paul established kingdom consulates throughout the region. The consulates provided classes on kingdom history, law, culture, and of course, immigration requirements. He appointed local kingdom consuls to assist new and prospective citizens. Every new citizen was strongly encouraged to consider a career in the kingdom Diplomatic Corps and to become an ambassador themselves.

Kingdom citizens who wanted to become ambassadors would meet with Paul or another ambassador who could set up a three-way meeting with the Prime Minister. The PM had the final authority in the matter. Often, the diplomatic credentials were slipped to the new ambassador by the PM before the meeting was over.

"Whether it is a large consulate or a small underground cell," Paul explained to his local consuls, "the mission is always the same: tell people about the kingdom, induct new citizens, train them in the ways of the kingdom, and get the word out to everyone on earth that the borders to the kingdom are opening—for kingdom citizens only."

Citizenship Application Deadline

Most people who responded to that message wanted to know the same basic things about the kingdom. The consuls, citizens, and ambassadors got a lot of practice distributing a consistent, understandable message.

They assured the people, "This is *not* a new program.[3] Israel's founding fathers looked forward to the arrival of the One to clear the way, so you can become kingdom citizens. For thousands of years, the Royals have been preparing a way for humans to cross over into the kingdom and to live forever! So give up your citizenship on earth, become a kingdom citizen and live, even after you die!"[4]

The consuls and ambassadors were peppered with questions from their audience, most of which were the same from day-to-day. They were ready with the answers.

"What do I have to do to get into the kingdom?"
"Come clean! Admit you have violated kingdom law. Publicly renounce Lucifer, the ruler of the earth and swear full allegiance to the kingdom of heaven and its Prince, Jesus. Do that and become a kingdom citizen.[5] That's it! All new citizens are given kingdom passports, and you will need that to get through passport control."

"Is it true that kingdom citizens live forever?"
"It is absolutely true, in the most real way possible, not some hopeful, wispy nonsense. We are talking about *real life*. The kingdom overlaps the dimensions of this earth and has dimensions you cannot see with human eyes, including time. Even when your earthly body drops away, you will live forever in the kingdom with a new body."[6]

"Aren't there other ways into the kingdom?"
"No! There is no other way! Anyone who wants to get in needs a kingdom passport!"[7]

"Can't we just focus on living our lives well on earth, and worry about immigration when we get there?"
"If you don't bother to get a passport when the passport office is open, what will you say to the immigration control officer? Know this, if you have been advised of the entry requirements and you ignore them, he will *not* let you in! Failing to apply for your kingdom passport is *exactly* the same as saying, 'I don't really care about entering the kingdom.'"[8]

"If we want a kingdom passport, do we have to give up everything we've worked for?"
"The building is on fire and you are more worried about your belongings than your life! Grab your passport first and run to safety, *then* think about your stuff!"[9]

"How can I even be sure my passport is valid?"
"If you find yourself knowing and following what Jesus told us, including telling others about the kingdom and encouraging them to apply for citizenship, that is a very good sign that your passport is valid."[10]

"But the men at the Justice Center tell me I can't qualify for citizenship!"
They are absolutely right, *you* cannot! But your substitute can qualify you! The lifeblood of Jesus that cleared your kingdom record is your pardon. All you need to do is accept the pardon and apply!"

Citizenship Application Deadline

"So I don't have to do anything?"
"You must publicly accept the pardon while you are on earth and apply to become a citizen of the kingdom. A pardon doesn't apply unless it is accepted by the one to whom it is offered.[11] No one can make you do it and no one is going to force you into heaven if you don't. But remember, the penalty for doing nothing is that you will be turned away at the border."

The ambassadors would always encourage the crowd to take action, *now*. "Decide one way or the other! No fence sitters! Dual citizenship is not acceptable! The Royals have *no* interest in only half of your loyalty.[12]

The kingdom's citizenship enrollment drive continued for many centuries. Citizenship rolls were growing, but response varied by region. In some places being a kingdom citizen became respectable and even fashionable; in others the local government made it punishable by death.

Either way, Lucifer knew that the Prince's immigration push was not going away anytime soon. "New times demand new approaches," he thought. "Let's see where I can stir the pot a little."

Alternative citizenship drives were held by citizens of earth. They pointed humans not to the Prince of the kingdom, but to "princes" by other names. While most of *their* followers say they know and respect Jesus, many of them were proponents of dual citizenship. Kingdom Department of Immigration policy does not allow issuing passports to anyone until they renounced all such rulers, other than the Prince of heaven and his kingdom.

Lucifer called out to whoever would listen, "Such intolerance! The kingdom of heaven isn't a monopoly and the Prince doesn't run the only game in town! There are a lot of choices and each one is as good as another! Take the best of each, but don't rush your decision. You've got plenty of time to decide."

In the middle of the main plaza of the great kingdom hall, the Prince spoke with General Michael. "Before we engage direct military action to take back the earth, I want a worldwide airdrop of leaflets directed at the civilians on the earth. Everyone on the planet must know the whole story of what I am offering, from beginning to end."[13]

"I want anyone, anywhere, to be able to pick up a leaflet in their own language and know what is about to happen and why. I want them to know how to protect themselves and their families," the Prince showed Michael a sketch of what he had planned. "Something like this …"

WARNING!
Here is the record of the Kingdom's dealings with earth…
Here is what is about to happen on the earth…
Here is how you can protect yourself and your family…
Here is what happens to those who ignore this warning…

FOR SHELTER AND PROTECTION:
Find any Kingdom representative and tell them,
"I want in!"

The prototype for the Prince's leaflets had been around for a while in the form of letters written by the first ambassadors. Those letters, combined with the books of the founders of Israel, covered all the points that the Prince wanted to make. Due to the limitations of printing technology, these leaflets had always been in short supply. That was about to change.

Citizenship Application Deadline

"Everywhere! I want them everywhere," the Prince said as he stood in Johann Gutenberg's print shop, in fifteenth century Germany. He gently flipped through the pages of the first mechanically printed Bible, his pre-production "warning leaflet."[14]

By the end of that millennium, printing presses were everywhere. On these presses, literally billions of copies of the Prince's warning leaflets had been printed.

"I don't want anyone on the planet to say they never heard," the Prince said to the PM.

"This is by far the most widely distributed publication in human history," the PM responded. "In thousands of languages, and more on the way! They will *all* hear about our citizenship offer, as long as they don't close their eyes and ears."

Lucifer felt like he was making progress as well, as the race for the allegiance of humans intensified. While mass murder had long been a fact of life on earth, the millennium closed with the twentieth century going down as the bloodiest hundred-year period in history.[15]

"The trick isn't simply wiping them off the planet," Lucifer explained to his soldiers. "It's getting them off the planet as clueless as possible about the kingdom and kingdom citizenship. As long as they are citizens of earth when they leave their bodies, the Prince can't have them, ever."

Lucifer, sounding like a coach at halftime, encouraged his troops. "Keep up the pace! We can't do much against the kingdom ambassadors who actually have the backing of the Prime Minister, but we can keep people away from them. Let's keep these humans occupied with themselves, with money, sex, power, real estate, good deeds, religious work, politics, their kids, with—well, with anything! I don't care, as long as they don't find time to apply for kingdom citizenship. And keep them away from those damned leaflets!"

"We will not back down! We have no reason to back down ... to hell with the Prince and his kingdom!" declared Lucifer.

Both the lower waiting room and the kingdom citizens' arrival lounge were processing an exponential increase in the number of deceased human souls.

Evacuation of Citizens

၄

"We held up our end of the transaction," the Prime Minister said to the Prince. "You fulfilled every term and condition, and paid the full price in accordance with the mortgage, and yet Lucifer continues to default."

"That's why the mortgage has penalty clauses," the Prince responded. "If that snake had even a single drop of honor, we'd never have to break the seals and refer to those sections."

"We all know this is not about the contract," the King interrupted. "For him it never has been. Lucifer knows he has never had a legal leg to stand on since you paid off the mortgage. This is personal. He is only out to hurt our family."

"Gabriel!" said the Prince. "Initiate the airlift. Recall all the ambassadors and evacuate our citizens from the earth. Get them out of harm's way, immediately!"

It was not a surprise but it was certainly a shock when the siren went off in the kingdom citizens' arrival lounge. It surprised some that General Gabriel was in the lounge, personally encouraging all kingdom citizens to, "Walk, not run, but walk to the lounge exit facing the border crossing." For now, *honorary* citizens of the kingdom from the old days would continue to wait in the lounge until the judgment.[1]

Everyone knew this day was coming, though it never seemed like it would be *today*. The citizens gathered outside the kingdom gate and waited, as the sirens wailed all along the secure border of heaven.

Citizens of the earth could not hear them at all, but the sirens from the kingdom were heard clearly all over the earth, by every single naturalized kingdom citizen on the planet.

It was the middle of the night for some, morning for others, mid-afternoon for still others. Each knew instantly what this meant. They jumped from their beds, dropped their work, stopped their conversations, screeched their vehicles to a halt, stood up at their desks, and looked up in the direction of the siren.

Many kingdom citizens on earth who heard the sirens were in the presence of citizens of earth. These friends, family and co-workers watched in awe as the kingdom citizens begin to shimmer. Expressions on their glowing faces looked as if they were seeing something absolutely amazing, *because they were*. They took a few steps up into the heavenlies, as if a whole new dimension or direction of travel had been opened to them—*because it had*. They approached the crowd gathering outside heaven's newest border crossing.[2]

Their citizen-of-earth friends watched as they simply vanished in an instant, without a trace and without a clue to where they had gone.

"Officials now believe that this is the largest case of alien abduction ever," was the unbelievable, yet seriously delivered network news report. Almost everyone thought that was preposterous, yet the "experts" on TV seemed to be convinced.

Evacuation of Citizens

Outside the gates of heaven, there was an instant reunion among kingdom citizens arriving from earth and those who had been waiting patiently in the citizens' arrival lounge.

The mother brought down by cancer, the nephew killed on the freeway, the childhood friend shot in the war ... They were all there, in perfect health and elated to see the new arrivals from earth! It was an unbridled atmosphere of celebration as families and friends were joyfully reunited.[3]

The gates of the kingdom proper swung open and the Prince came through into the happy throng. "It's time!" he shouted. "It's opening day! Come on in!"[4]

One by one, the crowd flowed through the hundreds of passport control lanes, as the kingdom immigration officers scanned each one for their kingdom passports. The officers were aware that everyone in this crowd was with the Prince, but they had a job to do and the Prince appreciated that. No one would get into heaven without a kingdom passport; it was their job to see to it.

The crowd poured into the great kingdom hall where a party and banquet had been prepared. Prince stepped up to the speaker's platform and addressed the multitude. "Ambassadors, consuls, citizens of the kingdom! On behalf of my father the King, and the Prime Minister who you already know, I officially welcome you to heaven!"

The crowd erupted in a cheer that shook the roof and sustained itself for a very long time.

The Prince was beaming. He stood on the platform, taking it all in, his eyes darting through the crowd, exchanging smile after smile. He knew every single one of these new citizens, and from the way they were hugging and shaking hands, it looked like a massive family reunion. Finally, the Prince raised his hands and the crowd quieted down.

"If anyone told you that the adventure is over, and now you are simply going to sit on a cloud with a harp, they—were—wrong!"

The crowd erupted in cheers again, ready to follow the Prince anywhere. The Prince gave a wink to the head harpist in the kingdom band, "Unless that's your job!"[5] The crowd cheered loudly for the band, as the harpists strummed a few chords in salute.

The Prince held up his arms and the roar of the crowd diminished a bit. "In accordance with kingdom law and with an agreement which was made over six thousand years ago in the garden colony, I have purchased back the earth for the kingdom." The cheers from the crowd surged. "But," he held his hands up again. "But, the warlord Lucifer has reneged on his agreement and has refused to step down as ruler of the earth."

The mood of the crowd suddenly began to turn. "I will now push him out," the Prince announced. In the span of a few seconds the crowd went from a noisy, cheering throng to an almost silent assembly.

"As I speak, forces of the kingdom of heaven are massing just inside the kingdom border, ready to unleash the awesome power of the kingdom's war machine onto the earth."[6]

The crowd was completely muted. Many of them had just left the earth that day. Most of them had family and friends who were still on the earth.

The Prince continued, "This difficult time on earth will be a last call for humans to renounce their earthly citizenship and apply for kingdom citizenship. During the next seven years, the earth will be under siege by the armed forces of the kingdom. *No one* will be oblivious to what I am doing. During that time, the Prime Minister will continue to send emissaries to enroll as many new kingdom citizens as they can, but the stakes have gotten extremely

Evacuation of Citizens

high. Humans who become citizens of heaven during this time will very likely be killed as traitors to the earth by their government and Lucifer's loyalist forces. We will receive these new citizens into the kingdom with honor."

The Prince's announcement had a sobering effect on the crowd as they became aware that the tensions and bloodshed which had been escalating on the earth for centuries were now being overshadowed by an even greater terror.

"It will be very bad for people on the earth, but my nation Israel will be protected through the storm as they always have been. Remember Noah, Joseph, Moses and the others? I was with Israel through their disasters then, and I'll stay with them through this one. You'll see. A Royal never takes back a promise!"

"This war will be over soon. When it is, we will return to the earth and for a thousand years. You will rule the planet with me, without the poisonous influence of Lucifer.[7]

"In the meantime, you all have much to see and learn in the kingdom. You may want to visit the Crystal Sea portal. From there you can observe all the events as they unfold on the earth. For now my friends, let's enjoy the kingdom together."

The Prince stepped down from the platform to greet his friends before leaving to meet with his generals.

Invasion! Last Call for Citizens
☙❧

General Michael and General Gabriel were just above the border crossing, going over last minute instructions with the commanders of their troops. They were ready for the assault.

The Prince strode into the great kingdom hall. His father, seated on his throne and surrounded by many attendants, was holding a sealed envelope which had just been brought up from the kingdom archives. It was labeled:

MORTGAGE
Terms for Buy-Back of the Earth

"Even though you have paid the full price to buy back the humans and the earth, Lucifer still refuses to vacate in accordance with the mortgage," the King said.[1]

"As we knew he would," replied the Prince. "I've done my part, so now we will hit him with the penalties for non-performance as spelled out in the mortgage….the envelope, please, Father."

The King handed him the thick envelope with the official seal of the kingdom office of land records on the outside.

"Michael! Gabriel!" the Prince called down to his generals, "I am about to begin opening the mortgage. Are you ready to execute the non-performance penalties?"

"We are ready, Prince!" the generals called back.

The mortgage envelope had another envelope within it, which contained yet another, and so on. Each had a kingdom seal on it and on the outside of each was written a mortgage term, and on the inside of each was written the penalty for non-performance on the mortgage. The kingdom army was about to enforce all the terms and penalty clauses.

The Prince broke the first seal on the mortgage, and a huge white horse with an armed rider bolted out of the army camp, through the kingdom border crossing, and galloped down toward the earth. He was intent on conquest, in accordance with the first penalty clause of the mortgage. The three-dimensional humans and the demons in the heavenlies had no idea what this multi-dimensional kingdom warrior was about to unleash.

Over the next seven years, one by one, the Prince opened the sealed envelopes, pouring out all manner of devastation on the earth. All the hallmarks of human civilization were systematically destroyed. The institutions of government, industry, commerce, agriculture, medicine, and law were decimated. The earth shook violently and even the skies above went dark. Millions of humans died. The vast majority of those who died were hustled into the lower waiting room, which was straining to accommodate the inflow.[2]

In spite of the chaos and carnage on earth, the Prime Minister was still issuing passports as fast as humans would

Invasion! Last Call for Citizens

publicly renounce Lucifer and apply for kingdom citizenship.

The Prince told the PM, "Time to get Israel into the fight." The PM and the Prince stepped down to the earth. The PM introduced the Prince to 144,000 humans from the nation of Israel—as the One promised to them some six thousand earlier in the Garden of Eden. They all pledged themselves to the Prince and became kingdom citizens.[3] They were immediately pressed into wartime service by the Prime Minister as special emissaries to encourage wartime immigration to the kingdom. It was a hard sell for some, given the political climate, but it was an easy sell for others, given the bleak outlook for the earth. More and more people were applying for and getting kingdom citizenship, in spite of the carnage going on around them.

These Israeli emissaries were working under the direct protection of the Prime Minister and not even Lucifer himself could touch them. Their message was very succinct: *"Last call for kingdom citizenship!"*

Everyone on earth knew that the kingdom was behind these devastating attacks, so a zero-tolerance policy was enacted by the government against anyone who renounced Lucifer and professed loyalty to the kingdom. Violators were executed immediately, publicly beheaded as traitors.[4]

"You can't hide the truth!" yelled a woman who had received her kingdom passport from the Prime Minister just minutes earlier. The authorities had been tipped off to her public renunciation. One man taped her hands behind her back and forced her to her knees while the other captured the gruesome scene on cellphone video.

"I watched my sister shimmer and disappear across the border into the kingdom," the woman screamed at the armed men. "Just before she vanished, the last thing she said was, 'I see Mom!'" It's true! Everyone is talking about it! You *know* it's true!"

Grabbing a fistful of hair, the officer shook her head violently. "You are a traitor! That kingdom of yours is killing our people! May your kingdom die with you!" With that he swung down a large machete and her body dropped to the floor.

Even before her assailants had left the room, a kingdom soldier picked the woman up out of her lifeless body and carried her to the kingdom citizens' arrival lounge, which was once again filling up with new citizens. As she sank into a chair, she heard, "Welcome to the kingdom, ma'am. You've been through a lot today, but it will get much better from here on out. May I get you a drink?"[5]

In heaven, the embankment of the Crystal Sea was packed. The immigrants from earth were shocked to see what looked like the end of their former civilization. They were in awe of the courage displayed by those who accepted the offer of kingdom citizenship despite the dire consequences.

Most of all, the new citizens looking down were amazed and saddened at the stubborn refusal of so many humans to accept the still-free offer of kingdom citizenship, even when it was clear to everyone that time was just about up for Lucifer and his earth.[6]

Suddenly, as the Prince opened the seventh sealed envelope, things got very quiet.[7] Onlookers in the kingdom thought perhaps the carnage was over. Michael and Gabriel's forces were simply letting the smoke clear a bit.

Many jumped back from the edge of the portal, as blinding flashes again rocked the earth. Mountains slid into the ocean creating massive tsunamis, wrecking thousands of ships. Nuclear plant meltdowns poisoned drinking water for millions.[8]

Whenever it seemed there could be no more devastation, more came. It was shocking that any humans were surviving on earth, but incredibly, many were somehow able to dodge the destruction.

"We need a leader who can rally the world against the Prince," Lucifer said. He encouraged Toman Darta, a brutal former dictator who had been in hiding, to come out and be that leader. Lucifer sent his troops to rally the support of regional leaders as Darta and his chief of staff, Blick Runson, prepared for a global telecast.[9]

CNN, SkyNews, Al Jazeera, BBC, France24, China Central TV, and the other networks that were still operating carried Darta's address, solidifying the image that Toman Darta spoke for all citizens of the earth.

"Fellow citizens, I want to be very clear with you. The terror that has rained down upon this planet is not the work of any citizen of earth. Rather, this unspeakable evil has come directly from the kingdom of heaven and its chief terrorists, the Royals. We must not allow anyone to live, not for a moment, who holds sympathy or loyalty to that despicable kingdom or its murderous rulers."

"In keeping up our global war on terror, the governments of the earth have expanded the cash bounty program for any citizen bringing proof of the execution of a kingdom citizen. You will be required to show some video or other evidence that they indeed renounced our benefactor Lucifer. By doing this you will be doing a great service to your fellow man."[10]

"Additionally, in order to restore order to the global financial markets, and to halt widespread corruption, I have ordered a transition to global cashless commerce. Dr. Runson will explain."

"Thank you President Darta. In order to halt runaway inflation, tax evasion, money laundering and currency speculation, we are instituting an all-electronic, globally-networked system of commerce. All it requires is the insertion of a simple chip," he held up his wrist to the camera, "There—you can barely see it—just a small mark to show it is properly installed." The mark looked like a tiny tattoo resembling three superimposed sixes. He continued, "All financial institutions worldwide are already linked with all merchant accounts, and regional currencies are all being converted to a single electronic currency, the LUCI. The LUCI will replace the confusing mix of dollars, pounds, euros, yuan, pesos, and a hundred other currencies. This conversion will give criminals no place to hide."

"Thirty days from today, cash transactions, and the corruption that comes with them, will be a thing of the past. Details of how to enroll are online." A web address flashed on the screen. "All police and fire stations worldwide have been equipped with the chips and everything needed for you to get yours installed. This program is not optional. Without the chip installed, you will not be able to access financial accounts or sell or purchase anything."[11]

"Hey, I thought Darta was dead," said one of the Crystal Sea onlookers. He was hanged for crimes against humanity. It was all over the Internet.[12]

"I thought so too," replied his friend. "But it looks like you and I are deader than he is."

"More dead and more alive!" he responded, as they gave each other a high-five.

After Darta had been supreme commander for three years, the LUCI and the electronic commerce system were faltering.[13] Darta was faced with an imminent collapse of the global electronic banking system.

"What the hell are we going to do?" he demanded of Runson.

Four television news networks playing on video screens in Darta's office were all reporting on the same disaster. What had started as a double spike in the global prices of gold and oil, had triggered a run on the LUCI.

"What kept the LUCI up was confidence in the system," Runson explained, quite sure that Darta knew what he was going to say. "This war on the earth by the kingdom has unified the people behind you, but they have all watched as our entire civilization has collapsed, right before their eyes."

"They watched us conjure up mountains of LUCIs with the click of a mouse to pay for the war, and in the process we destroyed the value of all their personal assets. Word is out that LUCIs are worthless, so nobody wants them!"

"I don't give a damn about their assets!" Darta bellowed. "They can't just abandon the LUCI! Make them use it!"

Looking out the window at the boiling clouds, Runson saw that he was not going to have time to address that problem.

The Prince thundered up to the great kingdom hall on his white horse and called, "Kingdom citizens from earth! Saddle up and follow me! You and I are going to put away the squatters!"

Members of the kingdom regular army brought white horses for all the new citizens. Each swung up into the saddle as if they had been doing it all their lives.[14] "This is awesome," said one new cavalryman to another.

The Prince's horse reared up and he shouted, "For the King!"

"For the King!" roared the response, as millions of former residents of the earth, along with kingdom regular army galloped behind the Prince down the kingdom road.

The armies of the earth had been expecting the Prince's assault, but they were no match for a multi-dimensional army falling down on them. It was like attacking a troop of blind men. They couldn't even see the Prince's army coming.

General Michael burst into Darta's office, and with both hands grabbed Darta and Runson by their collars and ran them straight through the plate glass window of his high-rise headquarters. He took them to a lake, which was much smaller than the Crystal Sea of heaven, but it was neither smooth nor crystal. It was a molten, sulfurous boil. General Michael threw Darta and his chief of staff headfirst into the lake.[15]

The Prince spotted Lucifer and made a direct line for him. He grabbed his former General by the neck while kingdom troopers bound him in chains. Lucifer was carried to the Pit as his rebels scattered. Just mention of the Pit threw them into a panic. As the kingdom security team lifted its cover, smoke poured from the Pit. The sound of vibrating wings from millions of killer locusts filled their ears.

"See you in a thousand years!" the Prince shouted as Lucifer was hastily thrown into the Pit. "Lock it up!" he shouted to his soldiers, who dropped the lid into place, sealing it in all dimensions.[16]

"Michael! Gabriel! Cease fire! We are finished down here," the Prince called out. "And tell the newest citizens in the arrivals lounge to join us. We want to greet them!"

Once again, Gabriel made an announcement in the citizens' arrival lounge: "All citizens of the kingdom who arrived in the past seven years, please join us now as we meet the Prince in the new garden colony on earth."

"All others, honorary citizens of the kingdom, please continue to relax here in the lounge. You will be seen by the judge in about a thousand years. Trust me, it will seem like only a day. Thank you."

The honorary citizens didn't mind the extra wait, since it seemed like they had just arrived a few minutes ago.

Reestablishing the Garden Colony

The citizen soldiers of the kingdom, formerly of the earth, gathered on horseback around the Prince, once more on the soil of earth. The kingdom regular army gathered behind them. It was over!

The excitement of victory was in the air. From a distance, they heard music. It was a parade of new kingdom citizens who had been killed on the earth in the war. As they came closer, the crowd heard the marchers singing patriotic kingdom songs.

"Make way for the newest citizens of the kingdom!" the Prince shouted, as Michael and Gabriel led the parade of martyrs down from the citizens' arrival lounge and back to the earth which they had so recently, and violently, left. At the same time, from another direction, the Prime Minister's 144,000 emissaries, kingdom citizens from Israel, joined the festivities.

The entire company of kingdom citizens broke into spontaneous cheering and joined in with the patriotic kingdom songs. The cheering went on and on as they celebrated their return to earth.

The Prince finally held up his hands for quiet, and the crowd went silent.

"This is our new home, for now," announced the Prince. "Every human who rode with me into battle today, down the kingdom highway, will rule with me here on the earth. And you who were killed for becoming kingdom citizens in the last seven years, you will rule with us! Now let's return the earth to the splendor that we enjoyed in the garden so long ago!"[1]

"But this time we're staying in the garden—" came a shout from the crowd, "*with you!*"

The Prince smiled and waved to the enthusiastic citizen as the crowd erupted in cheers yet again.

The kingdom Office of Foreign Affairs designated the earth as an unincorporated organized territory of the kingdom of heaven. This was an upgrade from its former unorganized status, now that the Prince and his co-regents were installed as rulers.

Many families started and grew large. People lived much longer; the population exploded and the earth repopulated quickly. In many ways it was much like the old garden. Under the Prince's reign and with his knowledge of agriculture, the ground of the earth returned to the fertile state of the garden, yielding many times more crops per acre than any of the humans had ever seen when they lived on the earth. Fish returned in abundance to the streams, rivers, and oceans, and ranchers watched over huge herds. There was plenty of food for everyone.[2]

The Prince was always in sight. He walked among the people and just visited, talked and laughed. "We're all family," he would always say, and he meant it.

Over time they were joined by citizens of earth who had survived the carnage of the war, but had still not become kingdom citizens. These somewhat shell-shocked refugees were also enjoying the peace and prosperity under the leadership of the benevolent rulers. Citizens of earth were

Reestablishing the Garden Colony

granted refugee status by the Prince on the condition that keeping the prime directive would be their first priority.

There is no kingdom policy that provides automatic granting of citizenship to the refugees, or to anyone in a kingdom territory; however, it was very easy to become a citizen since there were ambassadors everywhere and the Prime Minister was always pleased to preside over induction ceremonies. When they came of age, all persons born on the earth since the Prince's return still needed to personally renounce their citizenship on earth and apply for full kingdom citizenship, if they wanted to keep it as adults. They would then receive their own kingdom passport.

For whatever reason, many of them never found time to apply for kingdom citizenship. If one chose not to become a kingdom citizen, they were not compelled to do so. This was in accordance with long-standing kingdom policy for territories *outside* the kingdom proper.

The next thousand years was a time of restoration, growth, peace, and prosperity on the earth.

Back in the conference room in the great kingdom hall, the Royals and their generals held a quick status session.

"What's your question Michael?" the Prince asked.

"Sir, when you announced to the crowd that the earth was once again like the garden, that citizen shouted, 'This time we're staying!'"

"He did," replied the Prince with a smile, "and he really meant it."

"Well, *are* they staying?" Michael inquired. "The Prime Minister informed me that under the terms of the mortgage with Lucifer, it won't be long until he is released from the pit, back onto the earth. We all know what happened last time he met up with the humans."

"I am sure our kingdom citizens know Lucifer and his schemes well enough, especially since the PM is with them always; but for those who are still citizens of earth, the descendants of those who survived the great war, it *will* be the same as with Adam and Eve," the King said to the Prince. They could live in this peaceful garden of earth for a million more years; but they would *still* embrace evil when Lucifer shows up, just like in our first garden colony."

"What we are doing here is exposing Lucifer's great lie," the Prime Minister explained. "He has always whispered into human ears that it's the *social environment* or *corrupt governments* which are to blame for all the world's troubles. He encouraged the humans to, 'Pour your efforts into fixing those, *then* there will be lasting peace and security,' and that's *nonsense!*"

"You're right, PM," said the King. "The Prince gave the earth a perfect government and social environment for a thousand years. Michael, you just watch how many citizens of earth *run* to Lucifer and embrace him when he shows up."

"So, any change in plan to deal with that?" the general asked.

"No, we will not take away the right of humans to choose between good and evil. The plan stays the same—each human must choose," the Prince responded firmly. "We will continue to offer pardons and kingdom citizenship to the humans. Those who accept will be protected by the kingdom. Those who refuse—well, they are on their own."

Last Attack - Crushing Response

The era of peace and prosperity on the earth had been continuous for a thousand years since the victory celebration.

The Prince turned to Michael and quietly gave the order, "It's time. Let him out."

Silently, the kingdom border gates swung open. A kingdom Special Forces team headed toward the Pit. As the massive lid was lifted, acrid smoke poured around its edges and billowed into the sky. The officer yelled into the blackness, "Lucifer! Come out!"

"Damn!" Lucifer shot out from the depths of the pit, through the earth's three dimensions and into the heavenlies, as far as he could go. He breathed deep gulps of clean air and shook off the last of the clinging locusts.

For a very long time Lucifer had been planning what he would do upon his release.

"The real prize," Lucifer thought, "will be to seduce those born on earth in the past thousand years, after the return of the Prince. They had never been with the Prince in the kingdom proper, so just like Eve in the garden, they will be easy targets."

Anyone who had not yet made the commitment to become a kingdom citizen was a target for Lucifer. He needed to find a willing accomplice to deal with this opportunity.

Lucifer headed directly to the far-off home of Gog, an ancient enemy of the Prince who had survived the global destruction and chaos.[1] Although Gog knew how to get along in this postwar world, Lucifer was sure that Gog never liked playing the "prime directive game" with the conquerors from the kingdom. "Gog will be ready to listen," Lucifer thought confidently.

Gog was absolutely ready to listen. He was sick of playing the role of "humble vanquished human" before the Prince, but he was good at knowing which way the political winds were blowing. If there really was a chance to crush the Prince, or at least send him packing, Gog was in; but he told Lucifer that he doubted it could be done.

"His co-rulers are weak," Lucifer explained to Gog. "They took part in only that one battle, and mostly, they just watched the Prince fight."

"What about all the other people and their descendants? There are millions and most of them are kingdom citizens, aren't they?" Gog asked, knowing that he and the citizens of earth were greatly outnumbered.

"That, my friend, is the beauty of this plan," Lucifer smiled. "There are a *lot* of people who have still not committed to the kingdom. They aren't 'in' with the Prince as his co-rulers are. Every one of those people wants to make a name for themselves; and you Gog, will give them that opportunity to become leaders on earth." Gog nodded slowly as he thought. "What about the Prince?" he asked.

"He will never be in a weaker position," Lucifer lied convincingly. "He is fully occupied with his little family in the three dimensions of Jerusalem. Gog, I've looked at the numbers. Dimension for dimension, this will be a fair fight, except *you* will have the overwhelming advantage of surprise."

Lucifer knew full well that the Prince was active and powerful in all dimensions of the kingdom, making him absolutely invincible. He knew Gog and his army could never actually defeat the Prince, but this was Lucifer's chance to start all over again. Just like in the garden, where he won over Adam's wife, now he would trump the Prince by winning over the entire alien resident population of the earth; and maybe—*just maybe*—the rest would follow like Adam did, leaving the Royals without a human family.

Looking his newest friend in the eye, he asked, "So, Gog, are you in?"

"I'm in."

Gog and his army marched toward Jerusalem, recruiting more citizens of earth every mile, encouraging them to make a name for themselves, and step up to the challenge of real leadership. His offer appealed to the young men of earth. "The *privileged* ones rule with the Prince, but what about *you*? Come join us as we take our leadership positions in the government of our planet."

Not all the young citizens of earth were suckered in by the deceit, but many were. The army swelled in size, almost uncountable as they approached Jerusalem.[2]

"No more games," the Prince said quietly to his general, almost in a whisper. "Take them down."

Michael turned and shouted, "Fire in the hole!" Kingdom artillery showered down fireballs on the rebellious army, destroying every one of them before they reached Jerusalem.[3]

"The only way to handle evil," the Prince remarked, "is to kill it before it infects the city. We are not going through this again." Then he commanded, "Michael, take care of the source of the infection."

At Michael's direction, kingdom Special Forces scooped up Lucifer and carried him to the molten lake, throwing him in to join his friends Darta and Runson.[4]

"Damn you, Prince!" were Lucifer's final words as he hit the burning surface of the lake. Just as he had never been allowed to reenter the kingdom proper, Lucifer realized that there was now no hope of ever reentering the earth or the lower frontier. He was being bound in dimensional chains, now many dimensions below the gates of heaven, into a most miserable place.

"Anything else before we head to the courtroom?" the King asked the others in the conference room.

"Well, sir," Michael said, "We all know that this judgment has to happen exactly as planned, but only one thing concerns me."

"Tell us," encouraged the Prince.

"Most kingdom citizens on earth have loved ones in the lower waiting room, about to go on trial," Michael said. "Many will have a reason why someone or other down there should be let into heaven, even though throughout their life, that person consciously ignored or rejected all kingdom offers of citizenship."

The Prime Minister jumped in, "Look, Michael, a thousand years of peace and prosperity were just put at risk by a single hater of the King. Millions of alien residents in the lower frontier jumped up to follow Lucifer the minute he returned. There are *millions* in the lower waiting room who would bring poison into the kingdom by following their own desires instead of following the King. This last thousand years could not have made it any clearer."[5]

"Kingdom justice is perfect justice," said the King with finality. "Everybody gets what they want. Those who wanted to immigrate to the kingdom are in. Those who wanted to be free from the kingdom will get their wish. We respect every human's earthly choice to come into the kingdom, or to go their own way. I understand that some of our citizens could think it is a good idea to pull former friends into the kingdom—but I will not allow anyone to be dragged into the kingdom against their will, not by me, not by our citizens, not by *anybody*."

In the lower waiting room below the earth, conditions were worse than ever. After Gog and Lucifer's final attack, millions more citizens of earth had recently been jammed into those dark, crowded conditions. Even the video screens had finally gone blank.

In the kingdom citizens' arrival lounge, it was as pleasant as ever for the honorary citizens who were still patiently waiting.

Guests in both rooms would not have to wait much longer.

6: Judgment Day
Trial and Sentencing

"Escort the humans from immigration detention[1] into the defendants' arena," the bailiff instructed the kingdom deputy. "Immigration detention" was the kingdom's official name for Lucifer's old lower waiting room, where all the citizens of earth waited after leaving their mortal bodies.

The deputy called the detention center security station and passed the message.

A voice boomed through the detention center, "All citizens of the old earth are to report immediately to the high court of the kingdom!"[2] Automatic gates swung open and the court deputies escorted all of them into the defendant's arena. There were literally billions of humans moving from the lower waiting room into the massive courtroom in the Valley of Jehoshaphat. Each person had a story and they were ready to tell it to the judge.

As they moved up into the courtroom, all the lights in the lower concourse went out behind them.

In his melodious announcer voice, Gabriel advised the honorary kingdom citizens in the citizens' arrival lounge that the court was ready to receive them.

"There will be a lot of unsavory characters in the courtroom," Gabriel explained, "but we have a special honorary citizens' section to which you will be escorted."

The few citizens of earth who did not join Gog, those who had never applied for kingdom citizenship, were informed by the kingdom deputies that they were now considered to be aliens with no right to remain in the kingdom. They were brought up to join the throng in the defendant's arena.

All the kingdom citizens on the earth were escorted into the spectators' chambers of the courtroom, away from the earth. They didn't know it at the time, but they were evacuated from the earth for their own safety. Behind them, all the lights in the sky over the lower frontier went out. The only lights were in the courtroom.[3]

The Prince stood in his chambers at the door leading into the courtroom, waiting.[4]

"All rise for the judge!" called the bailiff. Billions of spectators and defendants rose to their feet.

A division of kingdom regulars under General Michael was already posted around the courtroom. The Prince strode through the doorway behind the judge's bench. Huge 4-D video screens above and behind the bench, and throughout the courtroom, made it possible for everyone in the room to see the judge, the speaker, and all the evidence.[5] This proceeding was to be a very public event.

The Prince, wearing a flowing judge's robe, paused before he sat and scanned the room. It was an awesome sight. Every human who had ever lived, who was not a kingdom citizen, stood in the defendants' arena. Each was as ready as they would ever be for their day in court before the Prince. Jesus swung himself down into the judge's great white throne.[6]

"The immigration and deportation tribunal for citizens of the old earth, in the jurisdiction of the kingdom of heaven, is now in session," boomed the bailiff. "The honorable Ambassador Extraordinary and Plenipotentiary to the Lower Frontier, former citizen of the old earth,

Trial and Sentencing

Prince of heaven, and high Judge of the kingdom, Jesus, is presiding. These proceedings are now in session." The bailiff hammered his staff on the floor of the main courtroom. It echoed off the high arched ceiling.

"Good morning all," said the Prince. Addressing those in the defendants' arena he said, "Citizens of the old earth! You are here today because you are stateless persons. Your homeland has been decimated by war. Judgment has already been carried out on Lucifer, your former leader. The government of the old earth is no more. As you are no doubt aware, kingdom immigration policy allows entry only to citizens holding kingdom passports. Without a kingdom-issued passport, entry is denied, and those without a passport are deported to exile alongside the leader of the old earth. Do you understand?"

The courtroom was dead quiet.

The Prince continued, "But this proceeding is a judgment, not a condemnation. Each one of you will be heard individually. As needed, this court is prepared to review all the evidence in your life, since every detail is a matter of public record." He rested his hand on a stack of books on his bench. The micro-data contained in those books detailed the events of the life of every individual who had ever lived on earth.

"In these proceedings, there is one subject of primary interest to the court: *While living on earth, did you consciously reject or ignore the opportunity to gain citizenship in the kingdom?*"

"If you did in fact ignore or reject that opportunity, then the other matters of your life will have no bearing on your judgment, so please spare the court explanations and lists of justifications, which do not have direct bearing on the subject of interest.[7] Also, this is not a hearing on the merits of the kingdom's long-held and widely published immigration policy—the need for kingdom citizenship in order to gain entry."[8]

"The Royal family, and I personally, went to great lengths to make pardons freely available, so you could be eligible to apply for kingdom citizenship. This information was widely advertised for thousands of years on the earth, through our kingdom consulates, embassies, and a leaflet-dropping campaign lasting more than five hundred years."

"This court will respect the wishes of those who have consciously rejected the kingdom's offer of citizenship, in favor of remaining a citizen of earth.[9] By the end of this proceeding, all citizens of the former earth will be escorted out of the kingdom to follow their ruler, Lucifer, into the lake of fire. They will never be allowed reentry into the kingdom."[10]

"The court is well aware of the possibility of mitigating circumstances. The court reserves its sovereign right to pass judgment, based on the merits of each case, consistent with kingdom law.[11] As an example, there are millions standing in the defendants' arena today who were killed before they were born, prior to taking a single breath on the earth. The wrath of this court is *not* reserved for you."

"There may be others upon whom the court will extend leniency within the law, but remember this—when you make your case before me," the Prince leaned forward over the bench, "I have very little patience for foolish excuses and lies.[12] All statements made in court will be reviewed against the evidence of the defendant's life on earth, as recorded in the books. Those sentenced to deportation will have been convicted by their own testimony."[13]

The judge turned his eye to the honorary citizens arena, smiling as he saw friend after old friend from as far back as before the great flood. "Finally," he said, "many here today received honorary citizenship in the kingdom before the arrival of the promised One. Your long-standing and often

Trial and Sentencing

long-suffering commitment to this kingdom is appreciated by the Royal family. I especially look forward to seeing you before my bench, and having the Prime Minister confer full kingdom citizenship upon you." He caught the eye of his oldest friend Adam, and gave him a personal nod and smile.

The Prince scanned the defendants' arena.

"There are a lot of people here today. When coming before the bench, the name of each defendant will be looked up in the register of issued and accepted pardons." The Prince placed his hand on the other book on his bench. "This is to ensure that no one is wrongly convicted and sentenced."[14]

Scanning the huge courtroom, the Prince was silent for a moment, preparing himself for a long session.

"Open the books of human deeds," he instructed, "and bring forward the first defendant."[15]

"Your honor, I bring before you ..."

And so began the great judgment of the citizens of earth, which did not end until the last human had been heard and received justice.

The Prince rose from his bench, turned to Michael and said, "It's time. Tear down that disgusting lower waiting room. Toss it all into the molten lake. Then incinerate the entire lower frontier, to clean out Lucifer's poisonous residue and make it ready for the new kingdom."[16]

7: Kingdom Comes to Earth
Immigration Project Debrief

In the great kingdom hall, there was a bustling of a different sort. Boxes were being stacked high outside the entranceways and piles of furniture were being hauled on carts across the shiny floor of the hall.

The King, the Prince and the Prime Minister sat around the conference table, along with Michael and Gabriel, in the only room that still had all of its furniture.

"Moving day!" announced the Prince, ready to assume the throne in his new, expanded kingdom in the lower frontier. The borders had officially been moved and the frontier had been formally annexed by the kingdom. The Royal city, New Jerusalem, was about to be established on the earth as the new capitol of the kingdom.

"It was a long time coming," said Michael.

"And costly," added the King softly. He looked at his son with intense pride. "Very costly."

"But worth it!" responded the Prince. "By the way, have you met my new family?" he said as he waved his hand toward the window overlooking the crowds of new citizens walking through the kingdom proper.

They all chuckled.

"So," the Prime Minister said, steering the conversation back to the original purpose of the debriefing, "the Immigration Project was a complete success."

Turning to his generals, the Prince said, "Michael, Gabriel, you and your troops were magnificent. Your service to the kingdom is appreciated beyond measure."

The generals nodded modestly and quietly thanked the Prince. "We are who we are because of you—*all of you*," Gabriel responded.

"Michael," the Prince asked with a wink, "do you think my people still see me as an ogre?"

Blushing at the reference to his comment from some seven thousand years ago, the general responded, "You demonstrated the purest love for them by what you did.[1] You proved that there was absolutely *nothing* you wouldn't do for them. They *saw* it. They know you're not—not an—um—ogre—sir."

The Prince smiled at the response from his uncharacteristically flustered general. Turning to the King, he said, "You reached out to them first, Father, and you sent me to bring them into the family—and they love you for it."[2]

"I didn't send just you, son. I sent you *both*," the King responded, with a nod to the Prime Minister.[3] "You two are quite a team."

They sat quietly around the table, enjoying the moment.

The Prime Minister was anxious to springboard the discussion on to the next topic. "Generals, I want to tell you about our next initiative. We will be taking the Immigration Project to a new level!"

Michael and Gabriel exchanged glances, both having expected at least a short break in the action. Gabriel took a deep breath, and said, "Never a dull moment in the kingdom. Please, tell us about it."

Immigration Project Debrief

There was a soft knock on the conference room door, and a mover stuck his head in. "When would be a good time to pack this room?" he asked.

The Prime Minister knew the Prince was anxious to move to New Jerusalem, so he deferred with a nod to the Prince. The Prince responded, "This would be a great time, thanks."

Standing up, the Prince looked at his generals and said, "Let's move to the conference room in New Jerusalem. The Prime Minister will tell you more about our next project when we get there."

The Prince smiled and asked, "Who wants to join me in heaven on earth?"[4]

The New Adventure

〜❧

"It's all new construction," the King explained to Moses as they looked at the plans spread out before them. "From the stars in the sky to the mountains and valleys on the earth."[1]

"And," interrupted the Prince, pointing to the sky, "here comes our pre-fabricated city. New Jerusalem covers almost two million square miles and reaches from the limitless power supply of the earth's outer core 1,200 miles down, to the upper floors which are actually above the earth's atmosphere—1,400 miles top to bottom, and the super-insulated walls are two hundred feet thick!"[2]

"The lower frontier is now officially part of the kingdom proper," the King announced. "The great Crystal Sea is no more, and our New Jerusalem is the last thing to pass through that portal."[3]

They all stopped, looked up, and watched as the entire pre-fabricated New Jerusalem settled into place on the refurbished earth,[4] sliding into a precisely engineered hole in the new earth. The city descended, as water from the old Crystal Sea gushed down the sides of the city, lubricating it as it lowered into place. It slid far below the earth and when it finally came to rest it would still extend almost two hundred miles straight up.

The citizens were shouting and cheering and crying all at the same time. The noise was incredible.[5]

"Look at those materials," added the prime minister as mile after mile of the city slid into its foundation. "Crystal, pearls, precious stone inlays everywhere. Even the streets are paved with semi-transparent gold."[6]

"So *that's* what you've been doing," Peter said to the Prince. "You said you were going to prepare a place for us, but this is outstanding![7] All it needs is a good place for fishing," grinned the big fisherman from Galilee.

"Check it out," said the Prince. "Not only do we have hundreds of miles of oceanfront, but also a river flowing down, right out of the throne room, through the city, out into the earth—and it is teeming with fish! If you get hungry while you're fishing, it has the Tree of Life on both sides of the river, giving delicious fruit all year long!"

The Prince's first friend Adam exclaimed, "*One* tree standing on *two* sides of the river! Like you said back in the garden, these extra dimensions are beyond what I could *ever* have imagined!"[8]

"Told you," said the Prince, grinning at his friends and fellow rulers of the new earth.

One of the citizens asked the Prince, "What do you have planned once we are all settled into our new city?"

The Prince smiled at him, put his hand on the man's shoulder and said, "Excellent. A man of action! Come, follow me and you will see …"[9]

Appendix 1:

Kingdom Passport Application Checklist

Passport Please - Second Edition

Kingdom Passport
Application Checklist
Page 1 of 2

KINGDOM OF HEAVEN
DEPARTMENT OF IMMIGRATION

Part A: Your Eligibility (Check one)

I was born on the Earth (Citizen of Earth by birth)	Yes ☐ No ☐
My father was born on the Earth (Citizen of Earth by bloodline)	Yes ☐ No ☐

If you answered "No" to either, this is the incorrect form for you.

Part B: Your Need for a Pardon (Check one)

I told a lie of any magnitude, ever	Yes ☐ No ☐
I stole something, large or small, ever	Yes ☐ No ☐
Had sex with someone who was not my spouse, or even thought about doing so, ever	Yes ☐ No ☐
Violated the prime directive* in any way, ever	Yes ☐ No ☐
Lived a relatively good life, gave to charity, performed public service, treated everyone with respect, parents were kingdom citizens	Not a passport requirement

If you answered "No" to all of the above, you probably made a mistake. Please recheck.
*Kingdom Prime Directive: "Total Allegiance to the King"

Part C: Your Willingness to Accept a Pardon (Check one)

I cannot pay for the consequences of having violated the prime directive of the kingdom, and know I need a qualified substitute to take my place	☐ Agree ☐ Disagree
I accept the pardon offered by the prince, with gratitude	☐ Accept ☐ Reject

You must answer "Agree" and "Accept" to receive a passport.

Appendix 1: Passport Checklist

Kingdom Passport Application Checklist
Page 2 of 2

KINGDOM OF HEAVEN
DEPARTMENT OF IMMIGRATION

Part D: Renounciation & Oath of Allegiance

I understand that dual citizenship is not allowed	Yes ☐ No ☐
I will publicly and permanently renounce my citizenship of earth and all allegiance to its ruler, Lucifer	Yes ☐ No ☐
I will pledge full allegiance to the Kingdom and its sovereign rulers, the Royals, and will demonstrate that commitment by the way I live my life, to the best of my ability	Yes ☐ No ☐
I renounce and turn from all my past actions which have violated the Prime Directive, and will ask the Prince and Prime Minister to help me live as a Royal should.	Yes ☐ No ☐

To be eligible for citizenship, all the above must be answered as "yes".

The above is a <u>checklist</u> for humans who desire to obtain a kingdom passport. It provides information on the application process and the guidelines for passport eligibility. To actually <u>apply</u> for kingdom citizenship and passport, you may contact the Royals directly, or see any kingdom citizen, consul or ambassador.

Check www.passport-please.com if you need help with this.

Kingdom Passport Office Hours: 24 x 7 x 365

Special Notice Regarding Office Hours: Due to escalating tensions between the kingdom and the administration of the earth, the kingdom passport office may close without advance notice.

Appendix 2: Endnotes

Passport Please is a novel. Every attempt has been made to follow the story, facts and spirit of the Bible. The characters in *Passport Please* say things that are not found in the Bible, but hopefully you will not find their words to be inconsistent with the Bible's message.

The references and notes that follow are presented to show the basis for the characters and plot elements in *Passport Please*, in order to help you come to your own conclusions.

Since *Passport Please* follows the Bible from beginning to end, these endnotes could have been longer than the book. What follows is by no means exhaustive or conclusive. Unless otherwise noted, Bible quotes are taken, with permission, from either the New International Version (NIV) or the New International Version, 1984 (NIV 1984).

Quotes from the Bible are in quotation marks. If a clarification was added inside the quotation marks by the author, it will be in brackets, for example:

Luke 8:31 "And they [the demons] begged Jesus ..."

For more information, see www.passport-please.com

Or contact us at info@passport-please.com

Quick Background on Citizenship

A person becomes a citizen of a particular country in one of three ways:

By **birth** - Anyone born in a particular nation has historically been guaranteed full citizenship in that nation.

By their **bloodline** - If at least one parent is a citizen of a certain nation, the child is eligible to be a citizen of that country, regardless of the country in which they are actually born, because of their bloodline.

Through **naturalization** - The transformation of a citizen who holds citizenship in one country, into the equivalent of a natural-born citizen of another is called naturalization. It often involves renouncing one's prior citizenship and allegiance, and taking an oath of allegiance to the new nation.

Quick Background on Diplomatic Positions

A **Prime Minister** is the most senior minister in the government. The prime minister selects and can dismiss members of the cabinet, and allocates government posts.

An **Honorary Consul** is a citizen of the country they live in, (i.e. an American living in the USA) who works voluntarily on behalf of a foreign country (like Uganda) to promote business and cultural relations between the countries.

A **Consul** is a citizen of one country (i.e. the USA) who works for his or her own government while living in a foreign nation (i.e. China) to promote business and cultural relations between the countries.

An **Ambassador** is a citizen of one nation, who is posted in a foreign nation, as the direct representative of the head of state of his or her home country. When an ambassador speaks, it carries the same weight as if the President of his or her home country has spoken.

Appendix 2: Endnotes

Introduction
Pages 1 to 3

[1] John 3:3 Jesus tells Nicodemus, "no one can see the kingdom of God unless he is born again."

[2] John 18:36 "Jesus said, 'My kingdom is not of this world. If it were, my servants would fight to prevent my arrest by the Jews. But now my kingdom is from another place.'"

[3] Since the 1970s, string theory has become an important field of study in physics. It bridges the gap between Einstein's theory of relativity (the physics of the universe) and Bohr's theory quantum mechanics (the physics of sub-atomic particles). String theory demands that there are at least eleven dimensions in the universe (length, width, height, time plus seven others). More information on dimensions and string theory can be found in the excellent and highly readable book, *The Elegant Universe*, by Brian Greene, (New York, Random House, 1999)

1: Judgment Day
Trial and Sentencing
Pages 5 to 10

[1] Ezekiel 28:17 "Your heart became proud on account of your beauty, and you corrupted your wisdom because of your splendor."

Isaiah 14:13-14 "You [Lucifer] said in your heart, 'I will ascend to the heavens; I will raise my throne above the stars of God; I will sit enthroned on the mount of assembly, on the utmost heights of Mount Zaphon. I will ascend above the tops of the clouds; I will make myself like the Most High.'"

[2] Rebellion in Heaven!

Revelation 12:7-8 "and there was war in heaven. Michael and his angels fought against the dragon [Satan], and the dragon and his angels fought back. But he was not strong enough, and they lost their place in heaven."

3. Lucifer (Satan), a leader of angels, was not always God's enemy. In the very beginning, he was a "team player" in the kingdom.

Job 38:4-7 "Where were you [Job] when I [God] laid the earth's foundation? ... while the morning stars sang together, and *all* the angels shouted for joy?"

4. Willfully renouncing or rejecting citizenship in the kingdom may be the "unpardonable sin."

Mark 3:29 "But whoever blasphemes against the Holy Spirit will never be forgiven; he is guilty of an eternal sin."

Luke 12:10 "And everyone who speaks a word against the Son of Man will be forgiven, but anyone who blasphemes against the Holy Spirit will not be forgiven."

5. Lucifer oversaw the Garden of Eden before being banished from heaven.

Ezekiel 28:12-14 "You were the model of perfection, full of wisdom and perfect in beauty. You were in Eden, the garden of God; every precious stone adorned you: ruby, topaz and emerald, chrysolite, onyx and jasper, sapphire, turquoise and beryl. Your settings and mountings were made of gold; on the day you were created they were prepared. You were anointed as a guardian cherub, for so I ordained you. You were on the holy mount of God; you walked among the fiery stones."

6. The presence of God has a distinct aroma. To some it smells like life, to others, it has the stink of death.

2 Corinthians 2:15-16 "For we are to God the pleasing aroma of Christ among those who are being saved and those who are perishing. To the one we are an aroma that brings death; to the other, an aroma that brings life."

7. Lucifer's rebel angels will face judgment.

2 Peter 2:4 "God did not spare angels when they sinned, but sent them to hell, putting them in gloomy dungeons to be held for judgment"

Appendix 2: Endnotes

[8] 1 Corinthians 6:3 "Do you not know that we will judge angels?"

There is a body of water between heaven and earth.

Genesis 1:6-8 "And God said, 'Let there be an expanse between the waters to separate water from water.' So God made the expanse and separated the water under the expanse from the water above it. And it was so. God called the expanse 'sky.'"

Just as we cannot see heaven, this body of water is not visible to humans under normal circumstances. But when the Apostle John was taken to heaven, he was given a view of what this sea above the sky looks like from there. Centuries earlier, the prophet Ezekiel looked up from earth and was allowed to see God's throne in heaven. He said it was like looking through a sheet of ice.

Revelation 4:6 (John saw) "before the throne there was what looked like a sea of glass, clear as crystal."

Ezekiel 1:22, 25-26, "Spread out above the heads of the living creatures was what looked like an expanse, sparkling like ice... Above the expanse over their heads was what looked like a throne of sapphire, and high above on the throne was a figure like that of a man."

God included a model of the Crystal Sea in the Jerusalem temple. It was a massive (11,500 gallon) pool of water that was actually called "the Sea." It rested *above* (not next to) twelve metal bulls, like the sea that is *above* the things of earth.

2 Chronicles 4:2-4 "He made the Sea of cast metal, circular in shape, measuring ten cubits from rim to rim and five cubits high ... The Sea stood on twelve bulls, three facing north, three facing west, three facing south and three facing east. The Sea rested on top of them."

Passport Please takes the position that the Crystal Sea is a defensive barrier between heaven and the earth, like a moat. Note that when God established this heavenly sea in the seven days of creation account of Genesis 1:3 through 2:3, he did not say, "it is good," as he did about all his other creations. This sea is more *necessary* than it is *good*. It is a necessary barrier, until evil is purged from earth at the end of the age.

Revelation 21:1 "Then I saw 'a new heaven and a new earth,' for the first heaven and the first earth had passed away, *and there was no longer any sea*."

To this day, Christians who commit their lives to Jesus Christ and come under his protection, mark their entry into the kingdom by passing through water—it's called *baptism*. That is a "picture" of passing through the Crystal Sea into the kingdom of heaven.

9\. Revelation 12: 9 "The great dragon was hurled down—that ancient serpent called the devil, or Satan, who leads the whole world astray. He was hurled to the earth, and his angels with him."

Revelation 12:4a "Its [the dragon's] tail swept a third of the stars out of the sky and flung them to earth."

Isaiah 14:12, 15 "How you have fallen from Heaven, O morning star, son of the dawn! ... you are brought down to the grave, to the depths of the pit."

2: Trouble in the Frontier

Establishing the Garden Colony

Pages 11 to 26

1\. The throne room in the great kingdom hall is a busy place.

Revelation 5:11 "Then I looked and heard the voice of many angels, numbering thousands upon thousands, and ten thousand times ten thousand. They encircled the throne and the living creatures and the elders."

2\. God's throne apparently has wheels.

Daniel 7:9b "His throne was flaming with fire, and its wheels were all ablaze."

3\. Isaiah 66:1 "This is what the Lord says: 'Heaven is my throne, and the earth is my footstool.'"

4\. *Passport Please* takes the position that after the earth was established in Genesis 1:1, a long time passed before the seven days of creation detailed in Genesis 1:3 through 2:3.

Appendix 2: Endnotes

Genesis 1:1 "In the beginning, God created the heavens and the earth."

After the earth was created, the Bible tells of an epic drama which played out in heaven and on earth. Lucifer, once highly regarded, turned against the King. He led the angels in a rebellion and was thrown to earth. (see note/page: 1/197, 2/197, 5/198, 9/200) This rebellion was followed by a devastating cosmic flood described in Genesis 1:2, leaving the earth and the heavens in need of a complete restoration.

Genesis 1:2 "Now the earth was formless and empty, darkness was over the surface of the deep, and the Spirit of God was hovering over the waters."

The Bible refers to this early flood and warns that just as "the earth of that time" ended with a cataclysmic flood, the "present earth" on which we now live will end in a cataclysmic fireball.

2 Peter 3:5b-7 "long ago by God's word the heavens came into being and the earth was formed [*in the "seven days" account*] out of water and by water [*from the cataclysmic flood of Gen 1:2*]. By these waters also the world of that time [*the original earth*] was deluged and destroyed. By the same word the present heavens and earth [*the world we know today*] are reserved for fire, being kept for the day of judgment and destruction of the ungodly. "

Some also point to geological science as evidence of a very long "time gap" between creation of the original earth and the seven days of creation account. "*The Bible, Genesis and Geology,*" by Gaines Johnson (2010, ISBN 145-1-54932-6) is a scientifically and Biblically sound guide to reconciling a literal interpretation of the Bible with the scientific discoveries of geology and the fossil record.   www.kjvbible.org

[5] Revelation 21:3 "And I [the Apostle John] heard a loud voice from the throne saying, "Look! God's dwelling place is now among the people, and he will dwell with them. They will be his people, and God himself will be with them and be their God."

[6] Ephesians 1:9-10 "he [God] made known to us the mystery of his will ... when the times reach their fulfillment—to bring unity to all things in heaven and on earth under Christ."

1 Corinthians 15:24 "Then the end will come, when he [Jesus] hands over the kingdom to God the Father after he has destroyed all dominion, authority and power."

Revelation 11:15 "The seventh angel sounded his trumpet, and there were loud voices in heaven, which said: 'The kingdom of the world has become the kingdom of our Lord and of his Messiah, and he will reign for ever and ever.'"

Isaiah 26:15 "You have enlarged the nation, Lord; you have enlarged the nation. You have gained glory for yourself; you have extended all the borders of the land."

7 Hebrews 11:3 "By faith we understand that the universe was formed at God's command, so that what is seen was not made out of what is visible."

Isaiah 44:24b "I am the Lord, who has made all things, who alone stretched out the heavens, who spread out the earth by myself"

8 Psalm 11:4 "The Lord is in his heavenly temple; the Lord is on his heavenly throne. He observes the sons of men, his eyes examine them."

9 Genesis 1:6-8 "And God said, 'Let there be an expanse between the waters to separate water from water.' So God made the expanse and separated the water under the expanse from the water above it. And it was so. God called the expanse 'sky.'"(see note 8, page 199)

10 Time is relative, not constant or universal.

2 Peter 3:8 "With the Lord a day is like a thousand years and a thousand years are like a day."

Psalm 90:4 "For a thousand years in your sight are like a day that has just gone by, or like a watch in the night." A "watch in the night" is generally regarded as four hours.

NASA proved experimentally that time moves forward at different rates depending on the relative speed of the timekeeper. In a 1985 experiment called NAVEX, a highly precise atomic clock flew on STS-61A/Challenger. Compared to an identical clock on the ground, the fast-moving clock measured a slowdown of time:

Appendix 2: Endnotes

0.000,000,000,295 seconds for each second of flight, an amount predicted exactly by Einstein's formulas. This amounts to a time difference between observers of 0.13 seconds over a five-day flight. See http://www.nasaexplorer.com.

Time measurement discrepancies between observers become *huge* as the relative speed between observers approaches light-speed. Then "hours" will pass for one observer while "years" pass for another, during the same period, *and they are both accurate.* Brian Greene, *The Elegant Universe*, (New York, Random House, 1999) chapter 2.

[11] Psalm 103:14 "he knows how we are formed, he remembers that we are dust."

Genesis 2:7 "God formed man from the dust of the ground and breathed into his nostrils the breath of life, and the man became a living being."

Leviticus 17:11 "For the life of a creature is in the blood"

[12] This conversation between the Prince and Lucifer is patterned after the conversation between God and Satan found in the Book of Job. After that conversation, Satan was allowed limited interaction with Job, to test the man's loyalty.

Job 1:6-12 "One day the angels came to present themselves before the Lord, and Satan also came with them. The Lord said to Satan, "Where have you come from?' Satan answered the Lord, 'From roaming through the earth and going back and forth in it.' Then the Lord said to Satan, 'Have you considered my servant Job? There is no one on earth like him; he is blameless and upright, a man who fears God and shuns evil.' 'Does Job fear God for nothing?' Satan replied. 'Have you not put a hedge around him and his household and everything he has? You have blessed the work of his hands, so that his flocks and herds are spread throughout the land. But stretch out your hand and strike everything he has, and he will surely curse you to your face.' The Lord said to Satan, 'Very well, then, everything he has is in your hands, but on the man himself do not lay a finger.' Then Satan went out from the presence of the Lord."

The name Job comes from the Hebrew for "hated." In the Bible, Satan is the only one we know who hated Job. Satan hates God and the humans who are made "in God's image."

Passport Please takes the position that what happened to Job is a "picture" of what happened to Adam, and the human race fathered by Adam. In our story, Satan asks God for permission to persecute Adam and Eve, and once Satan is authorized, he relentlessly pursues his targets, putting them through many trials.

Job, through his trials, demonstrated a persistent faith in God, and ended up being blessed more than he was when the trials began.

Job 42:12a, 16-17 "The Lord blessed the latter part of Job's life more than the former part ... After this, Job lived a hundred and forty years; he saw his children and their children to the fourth generation. And so Job died, an old man and full of years."

13 John 8:44b Jesus said regarding Satan, "when he speaks, he speaks his native language, for he is a liar and the father of lies."

14 Job 42:1-2 "Then Job replied to the Lord: 'I know that you can do all things; no purpose of yours can be thwarted.'"

Psalm 33:11 "the plans of the Lord stand firm forever, the purposes of his heart through all generations."

15 John 15:18 "If the world hates you, keep in mind that it hated me first."

16 Genesis 2:8 "Now the Lord God had planted a garden in the east, in Eden; and there he put the man he had formed."

Matthew 12:33 "Make a tree good and its fruit will be good, or make a tree bad and its fruit will be bad, for a tree is recognized by its fruit."

17 God lives and moves in other dimensions besides the ones with which we are familiar. Locked doors and angry mobs are not barriers .

John 8:23 "You are from below; I [Jesus] am from above. You are of this world; I am not of this world."

John 20:19 " On the evening of that first day of the week, when the disciples were together, with the *doors locked* for fear of the Jews, Jesus came and stood among them and said, 'Peace be with you!'"

Appendix 2: Endnotes

Luke 4:29 "They got up, drove him [Jesus] out of the town...in order to throw him down the cliff. But he *walked right through* the crowd and went on his way."

John 13:36 "Simon Peter asked him, 'Lord, where are you going?' Jesus replied, 'Where I am going, you cannot follow now, but you will follow later.'"

[18] Ephesians 2:6 "And God raised us up with Christ and seated us with him in the heavenly realms in Christ Jesus"

2 Corinthians 12:2,4 "I know a man in Christ [Paul, referring to himself] who fourteen years ago was caught up to the third heaven. Whether it was in the body or out of the body I do not know—God knows. [and he] was caught up to paradise. He heard inexpressible things, things that man is not permitted to tell."

[19] Malachi 2:15 "Has not the one God made you? You belong to him in body and spirit. And what does the one God seek? Godly offspring."

[20] Genesis 2:19 "Now the Lord God had formed out of the ground all the wild animals and all the birds in the sky. He brought them to the man to see what he would name them; and whatever the man called each living creature, that was its name."

[21] Modern physicists have identified at least eleven dimensions in our universe. All but three are invisible. (see note 3, page 197)

[22] Genesis 2:9 "The Lord God made all kinds of trees grow out of the ground—trees that were pleasing to the eye and good for food. In the middle of the garden were the tree of life and the tree of the knowledge of good and evil."

[23] Genesis 2:16-17 "And the Lord God commanded the man, 'You are free to eat from any tree in the garden; but you must not eat from the tree of the knowledge of good and evil, for when you eat from it you will certainly die.'"

[24] Genesis 2:24 "a man will leave his father and mother and be united to his wife, and they will become one flesh."

Ephesians 5:25 "Husbands, love your wives, just as Christ loved the church and gave himself up for her"

25. Psalm 115:16 "The highest heavens belong to the Lord, but the earth he has given to man."

Opposition and Legal Settlement
Pages 27 to 44

1. Eve misquoted the instructions God had given, and Satan pounced on her uncertainty.

   Genesis 3:2-3 (Eve speaking to Lucifer, who appeared as a serpent) "but God did say, 'You must not eat fruit from the tree that is in the middle of the garden, *and you must not touch it*, or you will die.' 'You will not certainly die,' the serpent said to the woman.'"

2. Genesis 3:4-5 "You will not certainly die," the serpent said to the woman. For God knows that when you eat from it your eyes will be opened, and you will be like God, knowing good and evil."

3. Rather than confessing a wrong, Eve rationalized her actions.

   Proverbs 30:20 "This is the way of an adulteress, she eats and wipes her mouth and says 'I've done nothing wrong.'"

4. Adam was not tricked by Satan. He knew what he was doing.

   1 Timothy 2:14 "And Adam was not the one deceived; it was the woman who was deceived and became a sinner."

5. Proverbs 1:7 "The fear of the Lord is the beginning of knowledge"

6. The Prince said he will send a "crusher" from the descendants of Eve, a human, who will destroy Lucifer.

   Genesis 3:15 "And I [God] will put enmity between you [Lucifer] and the woman [Eve], and between your offspring and hers; he will crush your head, and you will strike his heel."

   When God said "*your* offspring" to Lucifer, he was likely referring to offspring of the Nephilim from Lucifer's army, and their descendants. (see note 2, page 212)

7. Romans 6:23 "For the wages of sin is death"

Appendix 2: Endnotes

Ezekiel 18:20 "The soul who sins is the one who will die."

[8] Genesis 3:21 "The Lord God made garments of skin for Adam and his wife and clothed them."

Hebrews 9:22 "without the shedding of blood there is no forgiveness."

When God killed the animals in the garden and made coats for Adam and Eve, he established the consistent Biblical pattern for how the deadly consequences for human offenses (sin) can be taken by an innocent, willing substitute from their household. The animals were *innocent* of any wrongdoing (qualified to take someone else's guilt). As beasts of burden, they were *willing* to carry their master's burdens, and the animals were part of the human's *household*.

The "kinsman redeemer" pattern was made part of Jewish law in Leviticus 25, where a blood relative (*from the household, or kin*) who was qualified (*innocent of debt, he had the money*), could redeem someone's lost estate if they wanted (*they were willing*). A kinsman redeemer could "redeem" someone out of a situation from which they were unable to extract themselves. The animals killed in Genesis were prototype kinsman redeemers, extracting Adam and Eve from the death penalty.

Leviticus 25:23-28 "The land must not be sold permanently, because the land is mine and you are but aliens and tenants. Throughout the country that you hold as a possession, you must provide for the redemption of the land. 'If one of your countrymen becomes poor and sells some of his property, his nearest relative is to come and redeem what his countryman has sold. If, however, a man has no one to redeem it for him but he himself prospers and acquires sufficient means to redeem it, he is to determine the value for the years since he sold it and refund the balance to the man to whom he sold it; he can then go back to his own property. But if he does not acquire the means to repay him, what he sold will remain in the possession of the buyer until the Year of Jubilee. It will be returned in the Jubilee, and he can then go back to his property."

Joseph, son of Jacob, Genesis 37-50 is also a kinsman redeemer, sent ahead by circumstances to save his family and his nation from death. (see note 4, page 218) Boaz, the rich Jew in the book of

Ruth, also fits the pattern, as does Jesus, the ultimate kinsman redeemer .

Ruth 3:20 (Ruth speaking of Boaz) "That man is our close relative, he is one of our kinsman redeemers."

1 John 4:10 "This is love: not that we loved God, but that he loved us and sent his Son as an atoning sacrifice for our sins."

9. Hebrews 10:1,4 "The law is only a shadow of the good things that are coming—not the realities themselves. For this reason it can never, by the same sacrifices repeated endlessly year after year, make perfect those who draw near to worship ... It is impossible for the blood of bulls and goats to take away sins."

Hebrews 9:12 "He [Christ] did not enter by means of the blood of goats and calves; but he entered the Most Holy Place once for all by his own blood, thus obtaining eternal redemption."

10. Life after death for animals? The Bible does not give many details. We do know that God cares deeply for animals. He saved Noah and his family, along with the entire animal kingdom. After they disembarked from the ark, God declared *six times in a row* that he was making an everlasting covenant with humans *and* with every living being on the earth. He specifically called out domesticated and wild animals and birds. (Genesis 9:8-17)

Psalm 36:6b "Oh, Lord, you preserve both people and animals."

11. Genesis 3:22 "And the Lord God said, "The man has now become like one of us, knowing good and evil. He must not be allowed to reach out his hand and take also from the tree of life and eat, and live forever. So the Lord God banished him from the Garden of Eden to work the ground from which he had been taken."

12. Hebrews 9:27 "Just as man is destined to die once, and after that to face judgment"

13. Luke 4:5-6 "The devil led him up to a high place and showed him in an instant all the kingdoms of the world. And he said to him, 'I will give you all their authority and splendor; *for it has been given to me*, and I can give it to anyone I want to.'"

Jesus did not challenge Lucifer's statement of ownership of the earth, above; however, God said he is the ultimate owner of the

Appendix 2: Endnotes

earth and promises as our kinsman redeemer, to redeem the earth. (see note 8, page 207)

Leviticus 25:23-24 "The land must not be sold permanently, because the land is mine and you are but aliens and my tenants. Throughout the country that you hold as a possession, you must provide for the redemption of the land."

14   Ephesians 6:12 "For our struggle is not against flesh and blood, but against the rulers, against the authorities, against the powers of this dark world and against the spiritual forces of evil in the heavenly realms."

15   The plan of redemption to recover Adam's lost inheritance was written down. The seven-sealed scroll of Revelation contains the terms on which Adam's lost inheritance may be redeemed. This scroll is the "mortgage for the earth." M.R. DeHaan, MD, *35 Simple Studies on the Major Themes in Revelation,* (Grand Rapids, MI, Zondervan, 1946) page 94

The terms of significant land deals were written down and sealed.

Jeremiah 32:9-11 "so I bought the field at Anathoth from my cousin Hanamel and weighed out for him seventeen shekels of silver. I signed and sealed the deed, had it witnessed and weighed out the silver on the scales. I took the deed of purchase - the sealed copy containing the terms and conditions, as well as the unsealed copy."

The mortgage for the earth was kept safe in heaven until the time it was needed.

Revelation 5:6-7 "He came and took the scroll from the right hand of him who sat on the throne." "He" refers to "a Lamb, looking as if it had been slain."

16   Genesis 3:19 "for dust you are and to dust you will return."

17   Genesis 3:24 "After he drove the man out, he placed on the east side of the garden of Eden cherubim and a flaming sword flashing back and forth to guard the way to the tree of life."

18   Isaiah 28:24-29 "When a farmer plows ... [followed by a summary of instructions for plowing and planting cumin, wheat, caraway, barley, spelt, and grain] His God instructs him and

teaches him the right way. [more instructions on threshing and grinding grains, for bread] All this also comes from the Lord Almighty, whose plan is wonderful, whose wisdom is magnificent."

[19] Romans 3:23 "for all have sinned and fall short of the glory of God"

Romans 6:23 "For the wages of sin is death"

[20] The dead go below to a place known as Hades (New Testament), also known as Sheol (Old Testament). We know this is not the eternal heaven or hell, since its residents will come out from there.

1 Thessalonians 4:16b "the dead in Christ will rise first." (rise from the temporary Hades/Sheol, not from an eternal heaven/hell)

Revelation 20:13 "death and Hades gave up the dead that were in them"

Jesus described Hades as having two distinct zones— a comfortable one with cool drinks (also known as "paradise") and an uncomfortable one with fire and torment.

The early church father, Tertullian (160-220 AD), referred to the comfortable Hades as the "refrigerium interim." "Refrigerium" is the origin of the words "refreshment" and "refrigerator."

There is an un-crossable chasm between the two parts of Hades.

Luke 16:22-26 "There was a rich man who was dressed in purple and fine linen and lived in luxury every day. At his gate was laid a beggar named Lazarus, covered with sores and longing to eat what fell from the rich man's table. Even the dogs came and licked his sores. The time came when the beggar died and the angels carried him to Abraham's side. The rich man also died and was buried. In Hades, where he was in torment, he looked up and saw Abraham far away, with Lazarus by his side. So he called to him, 'Father Abraham, have pity on me and send Lazarus to dip the tip of his finger in water and cool my tongue, because I am in agony in this fire.' But Abraham replied, 'Son, remember that in your lifetime you received your good things, while Lazarus received bad things, but now he is comforted here and you are in agony. And besides all this, between us and you a great chasm has been set in place, so

Appendix 2: Endnotes

that those who want to go from here to you cannot, nor can anyone cross over from there to us.'"

The rich man realized his actions and attitudes in life are what put him in this awful place. He begged Abraham to warn his brothers, lest they end up in the same place.

Luke 16:27-31 "He answered, 'Then I beg you, father, send Lazarus to my family, for I have five brothers. Let him warn them, so that they will not also come to this place of torment.' Abraham replied, 'They have Moses and the Prophets; let them listen to them.' 'No, father Abraham,' he said, 'but if someone from the dead goes to them, they will repent.' He said to him, 'If they do not listen to Moses and the Prophets, they will not be convinced even if someone rises from the dead.'"

Abraham bluntly told him that anyone with access to the teachings of Moses and the Prophets (a Bible) already has the key to heaven; they just need to use it. He added that those who are unwilling to learn from Moses and the Prophets, are not likely to learn from "someone who rises from the dead," meaning, of course, Jesus.

[21] Faithfully offering blood sacrifices, as the Prince had instructed, secured a place in the kingdom for Abel.

Hebrews 11:4 "By faith Abel offered God a better sacrifice than Cain did. By faith he was commended as a righteous man, when God spoke well of his offerings."

[22] Psalm 90:4 "For a thousand years in your sight are like a day that has just gone by, or like a watch in the night."

2 Peter 3:8 "But do not forget this one thing, dear friends: With the Lord a day is like a thousand years, and a thousand years are like a day."

[23] Genesis 4:10 The Lord said, "What have you done? Listen! Your brother's blood cries out to me from the ground."

[24] An "outlaw" lives outside the responsibilities of the law; they give up the law's protections as well. This effectively gives the outlaw the same legal status as a wild animal. Richard Maybury, *Whatever Happened to Justice?* (Bluestocking Press, 2004) Chapter 6

25. God uses sarcasm on occasion when making a point.

Job 38:18, 21 "Have you [Job] comprehended the vast expanses of the earth? Tell me, if you know all this. Surely you know, for you were already born! You have lived so many years!"

26. God watches over his family, even when it is undeserved.

Genesis 4:15 "if anyone kills Cain, he will suffer vengeance seven times over.' Then the Lord put a mark on Cain so that no one who found him would kill him."

Locals Attack – Kingdom Response
Pages 45 to 50

1. Genesis 5:4 "Adam lived 800 years and had other sons and daughters."

2. Angels of Lucifer intermarried with women on the earth.

Genesis 6:1-2, 4-5a "When men began to increase in number on the earth and daughters were born to them, the sons of God saw that the daughters of men were beautiful, and they married any of them they chose … The Nephilim were on the earth in those days—and also afterward—when the sons of God went to the daughters of men and had children by them. They were the heroes of old, men of renown. The Lord saw how great man's wickedness on the earth had become"

3. Genesis 6:5,7 "The Lord saw how great man's wickedness on earth had become … I will wipe mankind … from the face of the earth."

4. Genesis 6:9 "Noah was a righteous man, blameless among the people of his time, and he walked with God."

"Blameless among the people," is more accurately translated from the Hebrew as "perfect in his generations." That refers to an unblemished family line, a direct descendant of Adam.

Appendix 2: Endnotes

5   Those in the lower waiting room can *see* across the chasm into the citizens' arrival lounge.

Luke 16:23 "In hell, where he was in torment, he looked up and saw Abraham far away, with Lazarus by his side." (original Greek is "hades," not "hell")

Luke 13:28 "There will be weeping there, and gnashing of teeth, when you *see* Abraham, Isaac and Jacob and all the prophets in the kingdom of God, but you yourselves thrown out."

Travel between the two sections of Hades (citizens' arrival lounge and the lower waiting room) is impossible.

Luke 16:26 "And besides all this, between us and you a great chasm has been fixed, so that those who want to go from here to you cannot, nor can anyone cross over from there to us."

6   Genesis 9:18-27 tells of Noah's episode of drunkenness, and how when he realized that Ham had gossiped about him to his brothers, Noah cursed his youngest son Ham, who then packed up and left.

7   Numbers 13 tells that hundreds of years after the flood, giant descendants of the evil Nephilim inhabited the earth—*but how?* All humans, except those in the ark, had perished in the flood.

Genesis 7:21 "Every living thing that moved on land perished—birds, livestock, wild animals, all the creatures that swarm over the earth, and all mankind."

Numbers 13:17, 32-33 "Moses sent them to explore Canaan… And they spread among the Israelites a bad report about the land they had explored. They said, 'The land we explored devours those living in it. All the people we saw there are of great size. We saw the Nephilim there (the descendants of Anak come from the Nephilim). We seemed like grasshoppers in our own eyes, and we looked the same to them.'"

Passport Please takes the position that a human of Nephilim descent was a passenger on Noah's ark. Most, if not all of the evil giants mentioned in the Bible are descendants of Noah's son, Ham.

In Genesis 10:15, "Canaan [Ham's son] was father of … the Amorites" In Amos 2:9, we learn that these Amorites were "tall as cedars." In Deuteronomy 3:1-11 we learn that one of the Amorite kings, Og, King of Bashan, was so tall, that his bed was 14 feet long and 6 feet wide. In Genesis 10:13, "Egypt" (another son of Ham, Genesis 10:6) was father of "the Kasluhites (from whom the Philistines came)," and the most famous Philistine in the Bible was a giant—Goliath.

1 Samuel 17:4 "A champion named Goliath, who was from Gath, came out of the Philistine camp. His height was six cubits and a span" (9 feet, 9 inches tall)

Ham's descendants also established or settled in Ninevah, Babylon, Assyria, Sodom, and Gomorrah (Genesis 10:10, 11, 19). These were all famous in the Bible as hotbeds of evil.

The places where Ham's family settled became known as evil lands populated by giants. One of Ham's sons was named Canaan. Hundreds of years later, when Moses sent spies to search out the land of Canaan (see Numbers 13, in this note), they found the land was populated with giants.

We know Ham's father, Noah, was of pure lineage (see note 4, page 212), but we are told virtually *nothing* about Ham's wife—not even her name. Based on the strong Nephilim-like characteristics exhibited by so many of Ham's descendants, *Passport Please* takes the position that Ham's wife carried Nephilim DNA onto the ark.

It is possible, though not mentioned in the Bible, that the "Sons of God" (Genesis 6:1-2) came to earth *again* to marry human women after the flood. *Passport Please* allows for that possibility (see novel, page 65).

Drawing the Battle Lines
Pages 51 to 56

[1] Genesis 11:4 "Come, let us build ourselves a city, with a tower that reaches to the heavens, so that we may make a name for ourselves"

[2] The earth is only temporarily turned over to Satan. God has the right to redeem it, or "buy it back." (see note 8, page 207)

Appendix 2: Endnotes

Leviticus 25:13 "In this year of Jubilee, everyone is to return to his own property."

Leviticus 25:49 "any blood relative in his clan may redeem him."

3   Concern would later be expressed, even by the angels in heaven (see note 2, page 233), that no one was qualified to fulfill or enforce the provisions of the mortgage.

Revelation 5:2-4 "And I saw a mighty angel proclaiming in a loud voice, 'Who is worthy to break the seals and open the scroll?' But no one in heaven or on earth or under the earth could open the scroll or even look inside it. I wept and wept because no one was found who was worthy to open the scroll or look inside."

4   The mortgage was held in a safe place for future redemption.

Jeremiah 32:14 "This is what the Lord Almighty, the God of Israel says: Take these documents, both sealed and unsealed copies of the deed of purchase and put them in a clay jar so they will last a long time."

Revelation 5:1 "Then I saw in the right hand of him who sat on the throne a scroll with writing on both sides and sealed with seven seals."

5   Unrestrained sexual activity is part of Lucifer's strategy. Humans can follow this path, and its consequences, if they choose.

Romans 1:24-26 "Therefore God gave them over in the sinful desires of their hearts to sexual impurity ... God gave them over to shameful lusts."

3: King's Academy
National ID System
Pages 57 to 62

1   Genesis 12:2 "The Lord said to Abram ... I will make you into a great nation"

Genesis 12:3 "all peoples on earth will be blessed through you."

2. Genesis 16:11-12 "The angel of the Lord also said to her [Hagar]: 'You are now pregnant and you will give birth to a son. You shall name him Ishmael, for the Lord has heard of your misery. He will be a wild donkey of a man; his hand will be against everyone and everyone's hand against him, and he will live in hostility toward all his brothers.'"

3. Genesis 17:17b "[Abraham] said to himself, 'Will a son be born to a man a hundred years old? Will Sarah bear a child at the age of ninety?'"

4. Deuteronomy 7:3 "Do not intermarry with them. Do not give your daughters to their sons or take their daughters for your sons."

5. Genesis 34 tells the riveting story of how Jacob's daughter Dinah was violated by a young man, in a region where most of the local men were uncircumcised. Her brothers took care of the offender, along with every man in his city, in an unusual and violent way.

6. While DNA from both parents contributes to establishing the traits of a child, the child's bloodline is established by it's father. In *The Chemistry of the Blood*, (Grand Rapids, MI, Zondervan, 1943) pages 30-32, M.R. DeHaan, MD quotes from *Williams Practice of Obstetrics*, *Nurses Handbook of Obstetrics*, *Howell's Textbook of Physiology*. All essentially say that the mother's blood has no contact with the baby in the womb, thanks to the placenta, also known as "the blood barrier." All nutrients pass through the blood vessel walls from the mother's circulatory system to the baby's system, but the mother's blood never mixes with the child's. They are completely separate circulatory systems.

    It should be noted that any person with a Jewish *mother* is considered to be Jewish. This view is rooted in Jewish tradition. With Mary as His mother, Jesus was undeniably Jewish, even while He is part of his father's royal bloodline.

7. Exodus 34:15-16 "Be careful not to make a treaty with those who live in the land; for when they prostitute themselves to their gods and sacrifice to them, they will invite you and you will eat their sacrifices. And when you choose some of their daughters as wives for your sons and those daughters prostitute themselves to their gods, they will lead your sons to do the same."

Appendix 2: Endnotes

8   God knew Israel would not obey his command to marry only within the nation. He even predicts it and writes a song about Israel's upcoming rejection of Him.

Deuteronomy 31:16 "these people will soon prostitute themselves to the foreign gods of the land they are entering. They will forsake me and break the covenant I made with them.'"

Deuteronomy 31:19 "Now write down for yourselves this song and teach it to the Israelites and have them sing it, so that it may be a witness for me against them."

The lengthy musical indictment of Israel's unfaithfulness (Deuteronomy 32:1-43) ends with the assurance that God will, in the end, save his people. God is not surprised by human unfaithfulness, and provides a way to escape punishment.

9   If the Father is of pure royal blood, then the child is pure royalty, regardless of the mother's bloodline.

Isaiah 7:14 "Therefore the Lord himself will give you a sign: The virgin will be with child and will give birth to a son, and will call him Immanuel."

Lessons of Loyalty
Pages 63 to 74

1   Genesis 22:1-18 is the story of Abraham almost sacrificing his son Isaac.

2   Jacob struggles with God, a characteristic of the nation of Israel.

Genesis 32:26 "The man said 'Let me go ...' but Jacob replied, 'I will not let you go unless you bless me.'"

Genesis 35:10 "God said to him, your name is Jacob, but you will no longer be called Jacob; your name will be Israel." (Israel means "he struggles with God")

3   1 Peter 5:8 "Your enemy the devil prowls around like a roaring lion looking for someone to devour."

4   The story of Joseph is in Genesis chapters 37-50.

M.R. DeHaan describes Joseph as a "picture" of Jesus. Rejected by his own people, he suffers undeserved punishment and ultimately welcomes everyone who will confess their guilt and accept his provision. See M.R. DeHaan, MD, *Portraits of Christ in Genesis* (Grand Rapids, MI, Zondervan, 1966) Chapter 22

Genesis 50:20 "You [Joseph's brothers] intended to harm me [Joseph], but God intended it for good to accomplish what is now being done, the saving of many lives."

5   Exodus 1:6, 11-13 "Now Joseph and all his brothers and all that generation died, but the Israelites were fruitful and multiplied greatly and became exceedingly numerous, so that the land was filled with them .... So they [the Egyptians] put slave masters over them to oppress them with forced labor, and they built Pithom and Rameses as store cities for Pharaoh. But the more they were oppressed, the more they multiplied and spread; so the Egyptians came to dread the Israelites and worked them ruthlessly."

6   Genesis 4:12 "When you [Cain] work the ground, it will no longer yield its crops for you."

7   Genesis 15:13 "Know for certain that your descendants will be strangers in a country not their own, and they will be enslaved and mistreated for 400 years." (prediction, looking forward)

Exodus 12:40 "Now the length of time the Israelite people lived in Egypt was 430 years." (fulfillment, looking backwards)

8   Exodus 1:22 "Then Pharaoh gave this order to all his people: 'Every boy that is born you must throw into the Nile, but let every girl live.'"

Exodus 2:3 "But when she [Moses' mother] could hide him no longer, she got a papyrus basket for him and coated it with tar and pitch. Then she placed the child in it and put it among the reeds along the bank of the Nile"

Exodus 2:10 "When the child grew older, she took him to Pharaoh's daughter and he became her son. She named him Moses, saying, 'I drew him out of the water.'"

Appendix 2: Endnotes

9   Communications between God and Moses through the burning bush is described in Exodus 3.

A "wormhole" is a dimensional "shortcut" from one region of the universe to another. See Brian Greene, *The Elegant Universe*, (New York, Random House, 1999) 265, 268

10   Exodus 11:5 "Every firstborn son in Egypt will die"

The story of the Passover is found in Exodus 11 & 12.

11   Exodus 13:21 "a pillar of cloud to guide them ... a pillar of fire to give them light so that they could travel by day or night."

Exodus 12:37 "The Israelites journeyed from Rameses to Sukkoth. There were about six hundred thousand men on foot, besides women and children."

The nation of Israel is estimated at 600,000 men, plus 600,000 women, plus 800,000 children—about 2,000,000 persons.

12   Exodus 14:5 "Pharaoh and his officials changed their minds ... 'What have we done? We've let the Israelites go and have lost their services!'"

13   Israel's escape through the Red Sea is described in Exodus 14:19-31. The exact location of the Red Sea crossing is a topic of much discussion. In 1978, American Ron Wyatt discovered Egyptian chariot wheels and other artifacts on the bottom of the Gulf of Aqaba (part of the Red Sea). www.wyattmuseum.com

The Egyptians trapped Israel on the west side of the Gulf, on the wide beach at modern-day Nuweiba. Mountains to the north and south, and only one entrance through the mountains from the west, left the Israelites trapped against the sea. (see map next page)

Ten miles across the Red Sea is the land of Midian, in modern day Saudi Arabia. Moses had raised a family in Midian (Exodus 2:15, 21-22). Crossing the Red Sea at this location was a homecoming for him. Before he had gone to Egypt to lead Israel, Moses sent his wife Zipporah to her father's house in Midian (Exodus 18:2). After Israel crossed the Red Sea and camped at Mt Sinai (see note 2, page 221), Moses was reunited with his wife.

Exodus 18:5 "Jethro, Moses' father-in-law, together with Moses' sons and wife, came to him in the wilderness, where he was camped near the mountain of God."

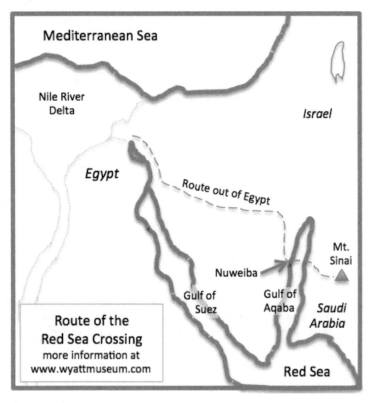

Law School
Pages 75 to 85

[1] "Manna" in Hebrew is translated as, "what is it."

Psalm 78:24-25 "he rained down manna for the people to eat, he gave them the grain of heaven. Men ate the bread of angels; he sent them all the food they could eat."

Appendix 2: Endnotes

Centuries later, Jesus compared himself to manna.

John 6:33-35a "'For the bread of God is the bread that comes down from heaven and gives life to the world.' 'Sir,' they said, 'always give us this bread.' Then Jesus declared, "I am the bread of life.""

2. Tradition places Mt Sinai in the south central portion of the Sinai Peninsula, in Egypt; however, the Apostle Paul tells us that Mount Sinai is actually across the Red Sea in modern-day Saudi Arabia.

Galatians 4:25 "Now Hagar stands for Mount Sinai in Arabia and corresponds to the present city of Jerusalem, because she is in slavery with her children."

Locating Mount Sinai in Arabia correlates with a Red Sea crossing at the Gulf of Aqaba. (see note 13, page 219)

3. Psalm 104:2 "He [God] wraps himself in light as with a garment"

Revelation 21:23 "The city does not need the sun or the moon to shine upon it, for the glory of God gives light"

1 Tim 6:15-16 "God, the blessed and only Ruler, the King of kings and Lord of lords, who alone is immortal and who lives in unapproachable light, whom no one has seen or can see."

Exodus 33:20 "he [God] said, 'you [Moses] cannot see my face, for no one may see me and live ... There is a place near me where you may stand on a rock. When my glory passes by, I will put you in a cleft in the rock and cover you with my hand until I have passed by. Then I will remove my hand and you will see my back; but my face must not be seen.'"

4. Exodus 33:11 "The Lord would speak to Moses face to face, as one speaks to a friend."

5. Deuteronomy 7:6 "For you [Israel] are a people holy to the Lord your God. The Lord your God has chosen you out of all the peoples on the face of the earth to be his people, his treasured possession."

6. The Ten Commandments are listed in Exodus 20:1-17 and again in Deuteronomy 5:7-21.

   Exodus 31:18 "When the Lord finished speaking to Moses on Mount Sinai, he gave him the two tablets of the covenant law, the tablets of stone inscribed by the finger of God."

7. Exodus 32:1-7 "When the people saw that Moses was so long in coming down from the mountain, they gathered around Aaron and said, 'Come, make us gods who will go before us. As for this fellow Moses who brought us up out of Egypt, we don't know what has happened to him.' Aaron answered them, 'Take off the gold earrings that your wives, your sons and your daughters are wearing, and bring them to me.' So all the people took off their earrings and brought them to Aaron. He took what they handed him and made it into an idol cast in the shape of a calf, fashioning it with a tool. Then they said, 'These are your gods, Israel, who brought you up out of Egypt.' When Aaron saw this, he built an altar in front of the calf and announced, 'Tomorrow there will be a festival to the Lord.' So the next day the people rose early and sacrificed burnt offerings and presented fellowship offerings. Afterward they sat down to eat and drink and got up to indulge in revelry. Then the Lord said to Moses, 'Go down, because your people, whom you brought up out of Egypt, have become corrupt.'"

8. Romans 3:20 "Therefore no one will be declared righteous in his sight by observing the law; rather, through the law we become conscious of sin."

9. Starting in Numbers 3, there is a detailed description of the construction and operations of the tabernacle, the "portable Justice Center." The tabernacle centralized the sacrifices, so they would be done correctly, and in order.

   Leviticus 17:5 "This is so the Israelites will bring to the Lord the sacrifices they are now making in the open fields. They must bring them to the priest, that is, to the Lord, at the entrance to the tent of meeting and sacrifice them as fellowship offerings."

Appendix 2: Endnotes

[10] By saving the firstborn from all twelve tribes of Israel in the Passover, God effectively "bought" their lives for himself.

Exodus 13:2 "Consecrate to me every firstborn male. The first offspring of every womb among the Israelites belongs to me, whether man or animal."

Numbers 3:39-48 details how God "traded" the firstborns he had saved, for the entire tribe of Levi. The Levites were then tasked with performing service in the Tabernacle, and later, the Temple.

[11] Matthew 22:29 "Jesus replied, 'You are in error because you do not know the Scriptures or the power of God.'"

[12] Deuteronomy 8:15 "He led you through the vast and dreadful desert, that thirsty and waterless land, with its venomous snakes and scorpions."

Numbers 11:14-15 "I [Moses] cannot carry all these people by myself; the burden is too heavy for me. If this is how you [God] are going to treat me, put me to death right now."

[13] Numbers 13:17, 32-33 (quoted in note 7, page 213) tells the story of the report of the spies sent into Canaan, including confirmation of Nephilim-descended giants in the land.

[14] Numbers 14:2-3 "All the Israelites grumbled ...'Why is the Lord bringing us to this land only to let us fall by the sword?'"

[15] Numbers 14:11-12 "How long will these people treat me with contempt? How long will they refuse to believe in me, in spite of all the miraculous signs I have performed among them? I will strike them down with a plague ... but I will make you into a nation greater and stronger than they."

[16] Numbers 14:15-16 (Moses to God) "If you put these people to death all at one time, the nations who have heard this report about you will say, 'The Lord was not able to bring these people into the land he promised them on oath; so he slaughtered them in the desert.'"

Numbers 14:17-18 "The Lord is slow to anger, abounding in love and forgiving sin and rebellion. Yet he does not leave the guilty unpunished."

Isaiah 1:18 "'Come now, let us reason together,' says the Lord."

17 Minors are not tried as adults in kingdom justice.

Numbers 14:28 "In this desert your bodies will fall—every one of you twenty years old or more who was counted in the census and who has grumbled against me"

Numbers 14:33 "Your children will be shepherds here for forty years, suffering for your unfaithfulness, until the last of your bodies lies in the desert."

18 Numbers 20:2-12 tells the story of Moses deciding to ignore God's directive to command the rock to yield water.

19 God always let Moses plead his case, but sometimes, even for God, enough is enough!

Deuteronomy 3:26 "'That is enough,' the Lord said. 'Do not speak to me anymore about this matter.'"

20 Deuteronomy 3:28 "But commission Joshua, and encourage and strengthen him, for he will lead this people across and will cause them to inherit the land that you will see."

21 Jude 9 "But even the archangel Michael, when he was disputing with the devil about the body of Moses, did not dare to bring a slanderous accusation against him, but said, 'The Lord rebuke you!'"

22 Moses couldn't lead the nation of Israel into the Canaan, but hundreds of years later he played a role in opening the way to an even greater promised land. (see novel, page 115)

School of Government
Pages 87 to 92

1 Joshua 1:4 "Your territory will extend from the desert to Lebanon, and from the great river, the Euphrates—all the Hittite country—to the Great Sea on the west."

Exodus 23:31 and Numbers 34:1-12 describe the boundaries of the Promised Land, from the Mediterranean Sea to modern day Iraq.

Appendix 2: Endnotes

2 Joshua 5:2-3, 7b-8 "At that time the Lord said to Joshua, 'Make flint knives and circumcise the Israelites again.' So Joshua made flint knives and circumcised the Israelites at Gibeath Haaraloth (Hebrew for "hill of foreskins")...They were still uncircumcised because they had not been circumcised on the way. And after the whole nation had been circumcised, they remained where they were in camp until they were healed."

3 Joshua 2 tells the story of Rahab the prostitute who helped Joshua take the city of Jericho and who later joined the family of Israel.

4 1 Samuel 8:7 "they have rejected me as their king."

5 1 Samuel 8:10-18 "Samuel told all the words of the Lord to the people who were asking him for a king. He said, 'This is what the king who will reign over you will claim as his rights: He will [*draft your sons into the army, put your daughters to work for himself and he will take what you grow and give it to his friends. He will take your servants and your livestock for his own use*] and you yourselves will become his slaves. When that day comes, you will cry out for relief from the king you have chosen, but the Lord will not answer you in that day.'"

6 In all of recorded history up to 1900 AD, an estimated 133,147,000 people were murdered by governments that were mostly, but not exclusively, totalitarian. This does *not* count war combatants. Then, in the 20th century, 169,198,000 were added to the number of those murdered by governments. R.J. Rummel, *Death by Government* (New Brunswick, NJ, Transaction Publishers, 1994), Chapters 1 and 2

7 The kingdom plan had always been (and still is) that the Prince would establish and head his government on earth.

Isaiah 9:6-7 "For to us a child is born, to us a son is given, and the government will be on his shoulders. And he will be called Wonderful Counselor, Mighty God, Everlasting Father, Prince of Peace. Of the greatness of his government and peace there will be no end. He will reign on David's throne and over his kingdom, establishing and upholding it with justice and righteousness from that time on and forever. The zeal of the Lord Almighty will accomplish this."

8. Circumcision could have protected the bloodline if only Israel had obeyed God's command not to intermarry.

1 Kings 11:1-3 says Israel's King Solomon, regarded by many as the wisest man who ever lived, had over 700 wives, a great number of them from foreign countries of which God had specifically said "do not intermarry with them!"

Ezra 9:1-2 "'The people of Israel, including the priests and the Levites, have not kept themselves separate from the neighboring peoples ... They have mingled the holy race with the peoples around them.'"

Ezekiel 16:26,28,29,32,60,63 "You [Israel] engaged in prostitution with the Egyptians ... the Assyrians ... Babylonia ... You adulterous wife! You prefer strangers to your own husband! ... Yet I will remember the covenant I made with you ... I make atonement for you for all you have done"

Malachi 2:11, 15b "Judah has been unfaithful. A detestable thing has been committed in Israel and in Jerusalem: Judah has desecrated the sanctuary the Lord loves, by marrying women who worship a foreign god ... he [the Lord] was seeking godly offspring."

9. Rahab the prostitute was an ancestor of Jesus, on both his mother and father's side. Matthew 1:5-16 details Joseph's genealogy. Luke 3:23-38 details Mary's genealogy.

10. In his attempt to "crush the Crusher," Lucifer was actually playing into God's hand. The Prophet Isaiah foretold that an innocent substitute would be punished, to pay the penalty earned by humans for their misdeeds, allowing justice to be fulfilled, and allowing humans to accept the pardon and go free.

Isaiah 53:5, 6b, 8b, 12b

> "he was crushed for our iniquities"
> "the Lord has laid on him the iniquity of us all."
> "for the transgression of my people he was punished."
> "he bore the sin of many"

Appendix 2: Endnotes

4: Reclaiming the Earth
Kingdom Head of State Arrives
Pages 93 to 100

[1] Luke 2:26b-29 "God sent the angel Gabriel to Nazareth, a town in Galilee, to a virgin pledged to be married to a man named Joseph, a descendant of David. The virgin's name was Mary. The angel went to her and said, 'Greetings, you who are highly favored! The Lord is with you.' Mary was greatly troubled at his words and wondered what kind of greeting this might be. But the angel said to her, 'Do not be afraid, Mary; you have found favor with God. You will conceive and give birth to a son, and you are to call him Jesus."

[2] Mark 2:1b-2 "Magi [wise men] from the east [likely from Persia] came to Jerusalem and asked, 'Where is the one who has been born king of the Jews? We saw his star when it rose and have come to worship him.'"

[3] Luke 2:13-15 "Suddenly a great company of the heavenly host appeared with the angel, praising God and saying, 'Glory to God in the highest heaven, and on earth peace to men on whom his favor rests.' When the angels had left them and gone into heaven, the shepherds said to one another, 'Let's go to Bethlehem'"

[4] Matthew 2:13 "an angel of the Lord appeared to Joseph in a dream … 'take the child and his mother and escape to Egypt … for Herod is going to search for the child to kill him.'"

[5] Mark 1:5 "The whole Judean countryside and all the people of Jerusalem went out to him. Confessing their sins, they were baptized by him in the Jordan River."

⁶ Renunciation of citizenship to one's old country and pledging allegiance to the US is a requirement for naturalized citizenship.

Baptism is the renunciation of one's old "country," and oath of allegiance to heaven and its ruler. See the similarities below.

US Oath of Allegiance: "I hereby declare, on oath, that I absolutely and entirely renounce and abjure all allegiance and fidelity to any foreign prince, potentate, state, or sovereignty of whom or which I have heretofore been a subject or citizen; that I will support and defend the Constitution and laws of the United States of America against all enemies, foreign and domestic; that I will bear true faith and allegiance to the same; that I will bear arms on behalf of the United States when required by the law; that I will perform noncombatant service in the Armed Forces of the United States when required by the law; that I will perform work of national importance under civilian direction when required by the law; and that I take this obligation freely without any mental reservation or purpose of evasion; so help me God."

www.uscis.gov, US Citizenship & Immigration Services

Church of England baptism liturgy:

Questions from clergy to the person being baptized:

Do you reject the devil and all rebellion against God?
Do you renounce the deceit and corruption of evil?
Do you repent of the sins that separate us from God and neighbor?
Do you turn to Christ as Saviour?
Do you submit to Christ as Lord?
Do you come to Christ, the way, the truth and the life?

www.cofe.anglican.org, Church of England

⁷ Luke 15:7 "I tell you that in the same way there will be more rejoicing in heaven over one sinner who repents than over ninety-nine righteous persons who do not need to repent."

⁸ James 4:4b "Anyone who chooses to be a friend of the world becomes an enemy of God."

Matthew 6:24a "No one can serve two masters."

Appendix 2: Endnotes

9   Matthew 3:15 "Jesus replied, 'Let it be so now; it is proper for us to do this to fulfill all righteousness.' Then John consented."

10   The fabric of Heaven was *torn* at Jesus' baptism.

Mark 1:10   "As Jesus was coming up out of the water, he saw heaven being torn open and the Spirit descending on him like a dove."

A *tear* in the fabric of space is the basis for a "wormhole," or bridge, connecting to new spatial territories. Brian Greene, *The Elegant Universe*, (New York, Random House, 1999) 265, 268

11   John 1:32 "Then John gave this testimony: 'I saw the Spirit come down from heaven as a dove and remain on him.'"

12   Jeremiah 8:6 "No one repents of his wickedness, saying, 'What have I done?' Each pursues his own course like a horse charging into battle."

13   God often speaks softly to his people—they need to listen to hear.

1 Kings 19:12 "After the earthquake came a fire, but the Lord was not in the fire. And after the fire came a gentle whisper."

Emergency Summit Meeting
Pages 101 to 103

1   Luke 4:1-2a "Jesus, full of the Holy Spirit, left the Jordan and was led by the Spirit into the wilderness, where for forty days he was tempted by the devil."

Isaiah 53:2 Jesus had "nothing in his appearance that we should desire him"

2   Luke 4:5 "The devil led him to a high place and showed him in an instant all the kingdoms of the world."

3   Luke 4:9 "The devil led him to Jerusalem and had him stand on the highest point of the temple. 'If you are the Son of God,' he said, 'throw yourself down from here.'"

4 Matthew 4:11 "Then the devil left him, and angels came and attended him."

5 Matthew 14:3 "Herod had arrested John and bound him and put him in prison because of Herodias, his brother Philip's wife"

Matthew 14:10 "and had John beheaded in the prison."

Offer of Kingdom Citizenship
Pages 105 to 116

1 Luke 4:16 "He went to Nazareth where he had been brought up, and on the Sabbath day he went into the synagogue, as was his custom."

2 Mark 1:22 "The people were amazed at his teaching, because he taught them as one who had authority, not as the teachers of the law."

3 Luke 4:17-21 "The scroll of the prophet Isaiah was handed to him. Unrolling it, he found the place where it is written: 'The Spirit of the Lord is on me, because he has anointed me to preach good news to the poor. He has sent me to proclaim freedom for the prisoners and recovery of sight for the blind, to release the oppressed, to proclaim the year of the Lord's favor.' Then he rolled up the scroll, gave it back to the attendant and sat down. The eyes of everyone in the synagogue were fastened on him. He began by saying to them, "Today this scripture is fulfilled in your hearing."

4 Luke 4:29 "They got up, drove him out of the town ...in order to throw him down the cliff ... But he walked right through the crowd and went on his way."

5 As noted on page 196, an Honorary Consul is a citizen of the country they live in, who represents a foreign country. (in this case, a citizen of earth representing the kingdom of heaven) After becoming kingdom citizens, they will become consuls, no longer "honorary."

6 John 1:47-48 "When Jesus saw Nathanael approaching, he said of him, "Here truly is an Israelite in whom there is no deceit.' 'How

Appendix 2: Endnotes

do you know me?' Nathanael asked. Jesus answered, 'I saw you while you were still under the fig tree before Philip called you.'"

7 Luke 17:20b-21 "The kingdom of God does not come with your careful observation, nor will people say, 'Here it is,' or 'There it is,' because the kingdom of God is within you."

8 Matthew 13:34 "Jesus spoke all these things to the crowd in parables; he did not say anything to them without using a parable."

9 Matthew 13:10 "The disciples came to him and asked, 'Why do you speak to the people in parables?' He replied, 'The knowledge of the secrets of the kingdom of heaven has been given to you, but not to them.'"

John 14:12 "whoever believes in me will do the works I have been doing, and they will do even greater things than these, because I am going to the Father."

10 Mark 8:29-30, "'But what about you?' he asked. 'Who do you say I am?' Peter answered, 'You are the Messiah.' Jesus warned them not to tell anyone about him."

11 Matthew 5:18 "I tell you the truth, until heaven and earth disappear, not the smallest letter, not the least stroke of a pen, will by any means disappear from the Law until everything is accomplished."

12 Mark 12:38-40 "As he taught, Jesus said, 'Watch out for the teachers of the law. They like to walk around in flowing robes and be greeted in the marketplaces, and have the most important seats in the synagogues and the places of honor at banquets. They devour widows' houses and for a show make lengthy prayers. Such men will be punished most severely.'"

13 John 10:38 "But if I do it, even though you do not believe me, believe the miracles, that you may know and understand that the Father is in me, and I in the Father."

14 Luke 5:18-26 "Some men came carrying a paralytic on a mat... When Jesus saw their faith, he said, 'Friend, your sins are forgiven.' The Pharisees and the teachers of the law began thinking to themselves, 'Who is this fellow who speaks blasphemy? Who

can forgive sins but God alone?' Jesus knew what they were thinking and asked, 'Why are you thinking these things in your hearts? Which is easier: to say, 'Your sins are forgiven,' or to say, 'Get up and walk'? But that you may know that the Son of Man has authority on earth to forgive sins ...' He said to the paralyzed man, 'I tell you, get up, take your mat and go home.' Immediately he stood up in front of them, took what he had been lying on and went home praising God. Everyone was amazed and gave praise to God. They were filled with awe and said, 'We have seen remarkable things today.'"

15 Again and again, Jesus told people to keep miraculous news to themselves—after Jesus heals a deaf man (Mark 7:36), after Peter tells Jesus that he (Peter) knows Jesus is the son of God (Mark 8:30), after Jesus heals a man of leprosy (Luke 5:14), after raising a girl from the dead (Luke 8:56), after explaining to his disciples about his upcoming death and resurrection (Luke 9:21).

16 Jesus taught that religious leaders can be dangerous.

Matthew 23:27 Jesus said, "Woe to you, teachers of the law and Pharisees, you hypocrites! You are like whitewashed tombs, which look beautiful on the outside but on the inside are full of dead men's bones and everything unclean."

Matthew 22:1 "Jesus spoke to them again in parables, saying: 'The kingdom of heaven is like a king who prepared a wedding banquet for his son. He sent his servants to those who had been invited to the banquet to tell them to come, but they refused to come'"

17 John 18:14 "Caiaphas was the one who had advised the Jews that it would be good if one man died for the people."

The high priest wanted to save Israel by getting rid of a troublemaker—he didn't realize that Jesus was *the One* sent by God, and his death would save *all* people who want to be saved.

18 Luke 9:30-31 "Two men, Moses and Elijah, appeared in glorious splendor, talking with Jesus. They spoke about his departure, which he was about to bring to fulfillment at Jerusalem."

In this scene, "the transfiguration," Moses and Elijah meet with Jesus to discuss details of Jesus' upcoming "exodus." In the NIV, "departure" is translated from the Greek word "exodos." An

Appendix 2: Endnotes

exodus from tyranny, as Moses led from Egypt, is descriptive of what Jesus was about to do—leading humans from the tyranny of Lucifer into the Promised Land of the kingdom.

[19] The kingdom plan, of which Peter had been unaware, was that many in Israel were "blinded" or "hardened" to the truth of Jesus' identity, as the promised One who would crush Lucifer's head and rescue the people of Israel. Jesus had been careful not to spread the word too obviously that he was "the One."

Romans 11:25-26 "I do not want you to be ignorant of this mystery, brothers and sisters, so that you may not be conceited: Israel has experienced a hardening in part until the full number of the Gentiles has come in, and in this way all Israel will be saved."

If the Jewish leaders realized that Jesus was the Messiah promised in their scriptures, it is unlikely they would have pushed for his death. Without the death of Jesus, humans would not be able to have their offenses (sins) paid for under kingdom law, and they would be barred from access to heaven. This "blinding" was for the good of humanity.

[20] Luke 9:34-35 "While he was speaking, a cloud appeared and covered them, and they were afraid as they entered the cloud. A voice came from the cloud, saying, 'This is my Son, whom I have chosen; listen to him.'"

[21] Mark 9:9-10 "As they were coming down the mountain, Jesus gave them orders not to tell anyone what they had seen until the Son of Man had risen from the dead. They kept the matter to themselves, discussing what 'rising from the dead' meant."

Completing the Transaction
Pages 117 to 126

[1] John 13:27 "As soon as Judas took the bread, Satan entered into him. 'What you are about to do, do quickly,' Jesus told him."

[2] God has mysteries, which he reveals selectively, as needed. Sometimes he reveals mysteries to a select few, who will share it widely later. Sometimes he reveals a mystery, intending that it not

be understood until later. Some of God's mysteries are hidden even from his angels.

1 Peter 1:12b "Even angels long to look into these things."

Matthew 24:36 "No one knows about that day or hour, not even the angels in heaven, nor the Son, but only the Father."

Ephesians 3:8b-10 "[Paul says I will] preach to the Gentiles the unsearchable riches of Christ, and to make plain to everyone the administration of this mystery, which for ages past was kept hidden in God, who created all things. His intent was that now, through the church, the manifold wisdom of God should be made known to the rulers and authorities in the heavenly realms"

Luke 18:34 "The disciples did not understand any of this. Its meaning was hidden from them, and they did not know what he was talking about."

Luke 24:15-16, 31 "As they talked and discussed these things with each other, Jesus himself came up and walked along with them; but they were kept from recognizing him." (hours pass) "Then their eyes were opened and they recognized him, and he disappeared from their sight."

3   John 8:23 "You are from below; I am from above. You are of this world; I am not of this world."

4   Mark 14:58 "We heard him say, 'I will destroy this man-made temple and in three days will build another, not made by man.'"

Acts 13:38-39 "Therefore, my brothers, I want you to know that through Jesus the forgiveness of sins is proclaimed to you. Through him everyone who believes is justified from everything you could not be justified from by the law of Moses."

5   No one person or group can be blamed for killing Jesus.

John 10:17-18 "I lay down my life—only to take it up again. No one takes it from me, but I lay it down of my own accord. I have authority to lay it down and authority to take it up again."

6   John 10:27-29 "My sheep listen to my voice; I know them, and they follow me. I give them eternal life, and they shall never perish; no one will snatch them out of my hand. My Father, who

Appendix 2: Endnotes

has given them to me, is greater than all; no one can snatch them out of my Father's hand."

7 Romans 8:2 "because through Christ Jesus the law of the Spirit of life set me free from the law of sin and death."

Galatians 5:13 "You, my brothers and sisters, were called to be free. But do not use your freedom to indulge the flesh; rather, serve one another humbly in love."

8 John 16:12-13 "But when he, the Spirit of truth, comes, he will guide you into all truth. He will not speak on his own; he will speak only what he hears, and he will tell you what is yet to come."

2 Corinthians 1:21b-22 "He anointed us, set his seal of ownership on us, and put his Spirit in our hearts as a deposit, guaranteeing what is to come."

Joel 2:28 "And afterward, I will pour out my Spirit on all people. Your sons and daughters will prophesy, your old men will dream dreams, your young men will see visions."

9 2 Corinthians 10:4 "The weapons we fight with are not the weapons of the world. On the contrary, they have divine power to demolish strongholds."

10 Ephesians 6:12 "For our struggle is not against flesh and blood, but against the rulers, against the authorities, against the powers of this dark world and against the spiritual forces of evil in the heavenly realms."

11 John 16:33 "In this world you will have trouble. But take heart, I have overcome the world."

12 John 14:26 "But the Counselor, the Holy Spirit, whom the Father will send in my name, will teach you all things and will remind you of everything I have said to you."

13 Matthew 26:26-28 "While they were eating, Jesus took bread, and when he had given thanks, he broke it and gave it to his disciples, saying, 'Take and eat; this is my body.' Then he took a cup, and when he had given thanks, he gave it to them, saying, 'Drink from it, all of you. This is my blood of the covenant, which is poured out for many for the forgiveness of sins.'"

Jesus said the bread and wine "is" his body and blood. He did not say that it "represents" his body and blood. His command for believers to participate in Communion is clear, but how the bread and wine of Communion allows believers to share in his eternal life, is a mystery. The Jewish leaders had difficulty understanding. So did Jesus' closest friends. In an earlier teaching on the subject...

John 6:52-53, 59-60 "Then the Jews began to argue sharply among themselves, 'How can this man give us his flesh to eat?' Jesus said to them, 'Very truly I tell you, unless you eat the flesh of the Son of Man and drink his blood, you have no life in you ... He said this while teaching in the synagogue in Capernaum. On hearing it, many of his disciples said, 'This is a hard teaching. Who can accept it?'"

Despite the above, Jesus did not chastise anyone for not fully understanding Communion. It seems that full grasp of *how* Communion "works," is not required, but faithful participation is.

14 The high priest demanded Jesus state clearly whether or not he was the son of God, and Governor Pilate demanded to know if Jesus was the King of the Jews. The gospels record that the answers Jesus gave were anything but clear.

To Pilate's question, Jesus responded:

> Matthew 27:11, Mark 15:2, Luke 23:3 "You have said so"
>
> John 18:34 "'Is that your own idea,' Jesus asked, 'or did others talk to you about me?'"

To Caiaphas, he responded:

> Matthew 26:64 "You have said so"
>
> Luke 22:70b "You say that I am."
>
> Mark 14:62 "I am"

"I am," above, appears to be a clear affirmative statement, but it had a provocative double meaning.

Exodus 3:14 "God said to Moses, 'I am who I am. This is what you are to say to the Israelites: "I am has sent me to you."'"

"I am" was the name by which God Almighty wanted to be known. With this answer, Jesus is not only saying he is the son of God, he

Appendix 2: Endnotes

is also saying he is God Almighty. To a Christian, that might sound reasonable, but to the high priest, "I am" was an incomprehensible, absurd and arrogant answer.

At this time, Jesus was not trying to help Pilate or Caiaphas know his true identity. He was on a mission, and he knew he needed to be put to death, as the prophet Isaiah predicted.

Isaiah 53:7 "He was oppressed and afflicted, yet he did not open his mouth; he was led like a lamb to the slaughter, and as a sheep before its shearers is silent, so he did not open his mouth."

[15] John 18:36 "Jesus said, 'My kingdom is not of this world. If it were, my servants would fight to prevent my arrest by the Jews. But now my kingdom is from another place.'"

[16] John 19:11 "Jesus answered [Pilate], 'You would have no power over me if it were not given to you from above.'"

[17] The crucifixion of Jesus is detailed in all four gospels:

Matthew 27, Mark 15, Luke 23, John 19

[18] Psalm 22:14-18 "I am poured out like water, and all my bones are out of joint. My heart has turned to wax; it has melted away within me. My strength is dried up like a potsherd, and my tongue sticks to the roof of my mouth; you lay me in the dust of death. Dogs have surrounded me; a band of evil men has encircled me, they have pierced my hands and my feet."

Isaiah 53:8b-10a "For he was cut off from the land of the living; for the transgression of my people he was stricken. He was assigned a grave with the wicked, and with the rich in his death, though he had done no violence, nor was any deceit in his mouth. Yet it was the Lord's will to crush him and cause him to suffer"

[19] Luke 23:39-43 "One of the criminals who hung there hurled insults at him: 'Aren't you the Christ? Save yourself and us!' But the other criminal rebuked him. 'Don't you fear God,' he said, 'since you are under the same sentence? We are punished justly, for we are getting what our deeds deserve. But this man has done nothing wrong.' Then he said, 'Jesus, remember me when you come into your kingdom.' Jesus answered him, 'I tell you the truth, today you will be with me in paradise.'"

The thief's *only* claim to kingdom citizenship was on a last minute citizenship application, direct to the Prince. "Paradise" which Jesus promised, refers to the comfortable Hades where the "dead in Christ" wait after death, not the eternal heaven ('kingdom proper' in the novel). (see note 20, page 210)

It is unlikely that the thief would have entered the kingdom proper (the eternal heaven) *ahead* of all the rest of the dead in Christ who are waiting for the trumpet.

1 Thessalonians 4:16 "For the Lord himself will come down from heaven, with a loud command, with the voice of the archangel and with the trumpet call of God, and the dead in Christ will rise first."

[20] Jesus dies alone on the cross, apart from even his father the King.

Matthew 27:46 "About the ninth hour Jesus cried out in a loud voice, 'Eloi, Eloi, lama sabachthani?'—which means, 'My God, my God, why have you forsaken me?'"

On the cross, Jesus had just quoted the Old Testament.

Psalm 22:1 "My God, my God, why have you forsaken me? Why are you so far from saving me, so far from the words of my groaning?"

[21] By January 1993, string theory had determined that space can indeed tear. When space tears, it can create a wormhole, or tunnel, to a distant part of the universe. Brian Greene, *The Elegant Universe*, (New York, Random House, 1999) page 280

[22] Jesus said that most people will miss the entrance to heaven, perhaps because most people are not even looking for it.

Matthew 7:14 "But small is the gate and narrow the road that leads to life, and only a few find it."

[23] Colossians 2:15 "And having disarmed the powers and authorities, he made a public spectacle of them, triumphing over them by the cross."

[24] In the womb, blood from the mother never comes in contact with the baby, thanks to the placenta, also known as "the blood barrier." (see note 6, page 216)

Appendix 2: Endnotes

Border Opens for Kingdom Citizens
Pages 127 to 129

[1] Jesus had told the thief that "Today you will be with me in paradise," referring to the comfortable part of Hades. (see note 19, page 237 about the thief and note 20, page 210 about paradise and Hades)

[2] John 15:15 "I no longer call you servants, because a servant does not know his master's business. Instead, I have called you friends"

[3] During his post-crucifixion visit to the underworld, Jesus went to the prison reserved for certain fallen angels.

1 Peter 3:18b-20 "He [Jesus] was put to death in the body but made alive by the Spirit, through whom also he went and preached to the *spirits in prison* who disobeyed long ago when God waited patiently *in the days of Noah* while the ark was being built."

Jude 6 "And the angels who did not keep their positions of authority but abandoned their proper dwelling—these he has kept in darkness, bound with everlasting chains for judgment on the great Day."

These "spirits in prison" are fallen angels who intermarried with women on the earth before the time of the flood, in the days of Noah. (see note 2, page 212) These disobedient angels are held in a dark prison until they face judgment.

2 Peter 2:4 "God did not spare angels when they sinned, but sent them to hell, putting them into gloomy dungeons to be held for judgment"

"Hell" in 2 Peter 2:4 is actually the Greek word "Tartarus." Used only this once in the Bible, the word Tartarus was mentioned in Homer's *Iliad* (c. 700 BC) as being, "As far beneath Hades as heaven is above the earth."

[4] Philippians 2:9-10 "Therefore God exalted him to the highest place and gave him the name that is above every name, that at the name of Jesus every knee should bow, in heaven and on earth and under the earth."

Psalm 22:29 "all who go down to the dust will kneel before him – those who cannot keep themselves alive."

5 1 Corinthians 6:3 "Do you not know that we will judge angels?

6 John 20:17 "Jesus said [to Mary], 'Do not hold on to me, for I have not yet returned to the Father. Go instead to my brothers and tell them, 'I am returning to my Father and your Father, to my God and your God.'"

The New International Version translation of Jesus' words, "do not *hold on* to me" is not precise. The original Greek is actually "do not *touch* me." The issue was not one of Mary *restraining* Jesus from his journey, but rather *defiling* the priest on his way into the "holy of holies." After the crucifixion, Mary had touched Jesus' dead body making her "ceremonially unclean." About to act as a "high priest" going into the presence of God, Jesus could not let an "unclean" person touch him until he had completely fulfilled his mission.

Numbers 19:11"Whoever touches the dead body of anyone will be unclean for seven days."

7 Hebrews 9:11-12, 24 "But when Christ came as high priest of the good things that are now already here, he went through the greater and more perfect tabernacle that is not made with human hands, that is to say, is not a part of this creation. He did not enter by means of the blood of goats and calves; but he entered the Most Holy Place once for all by his own blood, thus obtaining eternal redemption … "For Christ did not enter a sanctuary made with human hands that was only a copy of the true one; he entered heaven itself, now to appear for us in God's presence."

8 A very short time later, when Jesus had completed his work at the altar in heaven, it was no problem for Mary to touch and hug him.

Matthew 28:8-9 "So the women hurried away from the tomb, afraid yet filled with joy, and ran to tell his disciples. Suddenly Jesus met them. 'Greetings,' he said. They came to him, clasped his feet and worshiped him."

Appendix 2: Endnotes

5: Transition of Power
Local Resistance
Pages 131 to 144

[1] 1 Corinthians 15:40 "There are also heavenly bodies and there are earthly bodies; but the splendor of the heavenly bodies is one kind, and the splendor of the earthly bodies is another."

[2] Jesus walked in and out of human sight.

Luke 24:31 "Then their eyes were opened and they recognized him, and he disappeared from their sight."

[3] Luke 24:37-39 "They were startled and frightened, thinking they saw a ghost. He said to them, "Why are you troubled, and why do doubts rise in your minds? Look at my hands and my feet. It is I myself! Touch me and see; a ghost does not have flesh and bones, as you see I have.""

[4] John 20:22 "And with that he breathed on them and said, 'Receive the Holy Spirit.'"

[5] The Prime Minister of the kingdom will live inside you. He is your passport.

John 14:16-17 "I [Jesus] will ask the Father, and he will give you another Counselor to be with you forever—the Spirit of truth. The world cannot accept him, because it neither sees him nor knows him. But you know him, for he lives with you and will be in you."

Ephesians 1:13b "Having believed, you were marked in him with a seal, the promised Holy Spirit"

[6] 2 Corinthians 10:4 "The weapons we fight with are not the weapons of the world. On the contrary, they have divine power to demolish strongholds."

Ephesians 6:12 "For our struggle is not against flesh and blood, but against the rulers, against the authorities, against the powers of this dark world and against the spiritual forces of evil in the heavenly realms."

John 16:2 "They will put you out of the synagogue; in fact, the time is coming when anyone who kills you will think they are offering a service to God."

James 4:7b "Resist the devil, and he will flee from you."

7 Luke 24:49 "I am going to send you what my father has promised; but stay in the city until you have been clothed with power from on high."

8 Global deployment awaits those in kingdom service.

Acts 1:8 "you will receive power when the Holy Spirit comes on you; and you will be my witnesses in Jerusalem, and in all Judea and Samaria, and to the ends of the earth."

9 Matthew 28:18 "All authority in heaven and on earth has been given to me [Jesus]."

10 John 12:31 "Now is the time for judgment on this world; now the prince of this world will be driven out."

11 Before God returns to live in his garden, he will weed it, removing everything that is not authorized to be there.

Matthew 13:40-43 "As the weeds are pulled up and burned in the fire, so it will be at the end of the age. The Son of Man will send out his angels, and they will weed out of his kingdom everything that causes sin and all who do evil. They will throw them into the fiery furnace, where there will be weeping and gnashing of teeth. Then the righteous will shine like the sun in the kingdom of their Father. He who has ears, let him hear."

Matthew 25:31-46 tells more on the "weeding" process. "he will separate the people one from another as a shepherd separates the sheep from the goats"

12 Matthew 28:19-20 "Therefore go and make disciples of all nations, baptizing them in the name of the Father and of the Son and of the Holy Spirit, and teaching them to obey everything I have commanded you. And surely I am with you always, to the very end of the age."

Appendix 2: Endnotes

[13] John 3:3 "In reply, Jesus declared, "I tell you the truth, unless a man is born again, he cannot see the kingdom of God."

Citizenship in the kingdom is free.

1 Corinthians 2:12 "We have not received the spirit of the world but the Spirit who is from God, that we may understand what God has freely given us."

[14] Matthew 10:22 "All men will hate you because of me, but he who stands firm to the end will be saved."

John 17:14 "the world has hated them [Jesus' disciples], for they are not of the world any more than I am of the world."

[15] John 17:15 (Jesus prayed) "My prayer is not that you take [his disciples] them out of the world, but that you protect them from the evil one."

[16] Trouble comes when we get distracted from our mission, as Peter found out when he followed Jesus' call to join him in walking on the water.

Matthew 14:30 "But when he saw the wind, he was afraid and, beginning to sink, he cried out"

[17] John 10:28b Jesus said of those who commit to him, "no one can snatch them out of my hand."

Romans 8:38 "For I am convinced that neither death nor life, neither angels nor demons, neither the present nor the future, nor any powers, neither height nor depth, nor anything else in all creation, will be able to separate us from the love of God that is in Christ Jesus our Lord."

[18] The US Supreme Court decided in 1833 that the government has no power to force anyone to accept a pardon. To be effective, a pardon must be willingly accepted.

George Wilson had been sentenced to hang for his part in the death of a driver, during a stagecoach robbery. He was granted a pardon by President Andrew Jackson, but Wilson refused to accept it. The Supreme Court sided with Wilson, and he was hanged.

As part of the majority opinion of UNITED STATES v. GEORGE WILSON. U.S. 150 (1833), 32, Chief Justice John Marshall wrote:

"A pardon is an act of grace, proceeding from the power entrusted with the execution of the laws, which exempts the individual on whom it is bestowed from the punishment the law inflicts for a crime he has committed ... A pardon is a deed, to the validity of which delivery is essential, and delivery is not complete without acceptance. It may then be rejected by the person to whom it is tendered; and if it is rejected, we have discovered no power in a court to force it on him."

In the same opinion, Justice Marshall acknowledges that some may choose to refuse a pardon because the conditions attached to it are more than the recipient is willing to bear.

"A pardon may be conditional; and the condition may be more objectionable than the punishment inflicted by the judgment ..."

The conditions attached to God's pardon for humans are: renunciation of all allegiance to Lucifer, recognizing the need for a pardon, requesting that pardon and making a personal commitment to follow God to the best of one's ability. Many have decided that this price is more than they are willing to pay.

[19] Acts 2:1-4 "When the day of Pentecost came, they were all together in one place. Suddenly a sound like the blowing of a violent wind came from heaven and filled the whole house where they were sitting. They saw what seemed to be tongues of fire that separated and came to rest on each of them. All of them were filled with the Holy Spirit and began to speak in other tongues as the Spirit enabled them."

[20] 1 Corinthians 14:2 "For anyone who speaks in a tongue does not speak to men but to God. Indeed, no one understands him; he utters mysteries with his spirit."

1 Corinthians 13:1 "If I speak in the tongues of men and of angels"

Romans 8:26 "the Spirit himself intercedes for us with groans that words cannot express."

Throughout the history of diplomacy, ambassadors have been equipped with cryptographically protected communications

Appendix 2: Endnotes

capabilities. "Tongues of angels," spoken by humans, may carry messages which only God can understand. This is characteristic of a secure messaging system. Cryptography is used to hide the *contents* of important messages, but not to hide the *existence* of the messages themselves.

21 John 21:25 "Jesus did many other things as well. If every one of them were written down, I suppose that even the whole world would not have room for the books that would be written."

22 John 11:25b "He who believes in me will live, even though he dies; and whoever lives and believes in me will never die."

23 Philippians 3:20a "But our citizenship is in heaven"

24 Acts 3:6-10 "Then Peter said, 'Silver or gold I do not have, but what I do have I give you. In the name of Jesus Christ of Nazareth, walk.' Taking him by the right hand, he helped him up, and instantly the man's feet and ankles became strong. He jumped to his feet and began to walk. Then he went with them into the temple courts, walking and jumping, and praising God. When all the people saw him walking and praising God, they recognized him as the same man who used to sit begging at the temple gate called Beautiful, and they were filled with wonder and amazement at what had happened to him."

25 Jesus was not murdered or killed. He willingly gave up his life.

John 10:17-18 "The reason my Father loves me is that I lay down my life—only to take it up again. No one takes it from me, but I lay it down of my own accord. I have authority to lay it down and authority to take it up again."

26 Acts 4:4 "But many who heard the message believed and the number of men grew to about five thousand."

27 Acts 4:3 "They seized Peter and John, and because it was evening, they put them in jail until the next day."

28 Acts 5:31 "God exalted him to his own right hand as Prince and Savior that he might give repentance and forgiveness of sins to Israel."

Peter is an ambassador, speaking boldly as an ambassador would, with all the authority of the kingdom of heaven.

2 Corinthians 5:20a "We are therefore Christ's ambassadors ..."

Acts 4:8-12 "Then Peter, filled with the Holy Spirit, said to them: 'Rulers and elders of the people! If we are being called to account today for an act of kindness shown to a cripple and are asked how he was healed, then know this, you and all the people of Israel: It is by the name of Jesus Christ of Nazareth, whom you crucified but whom God raised from the dead, that this man stands before you healed. He is 'the stone you builders rejected, which has become the capstone.' [from Psalm 118:22] Salvation is found in no one else, for there is no other name under heaven given to men by which we must be saved.'"

29. Acts 4:13-17 "When they saw the courage of Peter and John and realized that they were unschooled, ordinary men, they were astonished and they took note that these men had been with Jesus. But since they could see the man who had been healed standing there with them, there was nothing they could say. So they ordered them to withdraw from the Sanhedrin and then conferred together. 'What are we going to do with these men?' they asked. 'Everybody living in Jerusalem knows they have done an outstanding miracle, and we cannot deny it. But to stop this thing from spreading any further among the people, we must warn these men to speak no longer to anyone in this name.'"

30. The Royals are determined to take back the earth and the humans who will come.

Matthew 11:12 "From the days of John the Baptist until now, the kingdom of heaven has been forcefully advancing, and forceful men lay hold of it."

Citizenship Application Deadline
Pages 145 to 154

1. Acts 5:12b-13a "all the believers used to meet together in Solomon's Colonnade. No one else dared join them"

Appendix 2: Endnotes

2   Acts 9:3-6 "As he neared Damascus on his journey, suddenly a light from heaven flashed around him. He fell to the ground and heard a voice say to him, 'Saul, Saul, why do you persecute me?' 'Who are you, Lord?' Saul asked. 'I am Jesus, whom you are persecuting," he replied. 'Now get up and go into the city, and you will be told what you must do.'"

3   Matthew 5:17 "Do not think that I [Jesus] have come to abolish the Law or the Prophets; I have not come to abolish them but to fulfill them."

4   John 11:25 "Jesus said to her [Martha, sister of his friend Lazarus], "I am the resurrection and the life. The one who believes in me will live, even though they die"

5   Romans 10:9 "if you confess with your mouth, 'Jesus is Lord,' and believe in your heart that God raised him from the dead, you will be saved."

6   John 11:25 "He who believes in me will live, even through he dies."

Philippians 3:21 "[Jesus] who, by the power that enables him to bring everything under his control, will transform our lowly bodies so that they will be like his glorious body."

1 John 3:2 "Dear friends, now we are children of God, and what we will be has not yet been made known. But we know that when he appears, we shall be like him, for we shall see him as he is."

7   Jesus provided the only way to heaven. If there was another way, Jesus was foolish or deluded because he could have avoided a senseless, gruesome death by simply pointing it out.

John 14:6 "I am the way and the truth and the life. No one comes to the Father except through me."

8   Ignoring the clear requirements for entry into heaven will have consequences at heaven's gates.

Luke 9:26, "If anyone is ashamed of me and my words, the Son of Man will be ashamed of him when he comes in his glory and in the glory of the Father and of the holy angels."

Luke 12:9 "But he who disowns me before men will be disowned before the angels of God."

2 Peter 2:21 "It would have been better for them not to have known the way of righteousness, than to have known it and then to turn their backs on the sacred command that was passed on to them."

Luke 10:16 "he who rejects me [Jesus] rejects him who sent me."

9. Matthew 6:33 "But seek first his kingdom and his righteousness, and all these things will be given to you as well."

Luke 12:34 "For where your treasure is, there your heart will be also."

10. John 14:21 "Whoever has my commands and obeys them, he is the one who loves me. He who loves me will be loved by my Father, and I too will love him and show myself to him."

John 14:23-24 "Jesus replied, 'Anyone who loves me will obey my teaching. My Father will love them, and we will come to them and make our home with them. Anyone who does not love me will not obey my teaching. These words you hear are not my own; they belong to the Father who sent me.'"

11. If one does not actually accept the pardon which is offered to them, the pardon has no value. (see note 18, page 243)

12. *Today* is the day. No one is promised tomorrow—so choose *now*.

1 Chronicles 29:5 "Now, who is willing to consecrate himself today to the Lord?"

Luke 12:19-20 (the rich man said) "And I'll say to myself, 'You have plenty of good things laid up for many years. Take life easy; eat, drink and be merry.' But God said to him, 'You fool! This very night your life will be demanded from you.'"

Matthew 6:24 "No one can serve two masters. Either he will hate the one and love the other, or he will be devoted to the one and despise the other."

Revelation 3:16 "So, because you are lukewarm—neither hot nor cold—I am about to spit you out of my mouth."

Appendix 2: Endnotes

[13] A nation which is about to invade another will often drop leaflets as a warning to the general population as well as enemy combatants, regarding the invasion to come and instructions on how to find safety.

In the 2006 Israel-Lebanon conflict, Israel dropped huge numbers of leaflets on southern Lebanon prior to initiating hostilities. These leaflets provided warnings regarding the enemy:

> *"Terrorists are operating in your area, and you are being exploited as 'human shields'"*

About Israel's plans:

> *"The Israel Defense Force will intensify its activities and will heavily bomb the entire area from which rockets are being launched"*

About what behavior will put one in danger:

> *"anyone traveling in a pickup truck or truck is endangering his life"*

And instructions on how to find safety:

> *"evacuate your villages and move north of the Litani River"*

From www.mfa.gov.il, Israel Ministry of Foreign Affairs

The Bible serves as such a leaflet, disclosing to everyone on the planet, the nature and identity of the enemy, the intentions of the kingdom of heaven and its rulers, the behaviors which will put one in danger, and instructions on how to find safety.

[14] Johann Gutenberg (1400-1468) invented the mechanical printing press. The first book printed was 180 copies of the Bible. The most widely distributed and translated book on the planet, by the end of the 20th century the number of Bibles sold exceeded one billion, in over 2,000 languages. Josh McDowell, *The New Evidence that Demands a Verdict,* (Thomas Nelson, Nashville, 1999) page 8

[15] The earth has a bloody history and the carnage is accelerating... In the 20th century, there were over 203,000,000 persons killed by war and government actions. This is more than a 20% increase in the estimated number from *all* prior recorded history combined. R.J. Rummel, Death by Government (New Brunswick, NJ, Transaction Publishers, 1994), Chapters 1-3

Evacuation of Citizens
Pages 155 to 159

[1] The "righteous dead" who were committed to the kingdom but did not know Jesus, will rise later. Abraham, who was in "paradise" with Lazarus, is an example of such a person (see note 20, page 210).

1 Thessalonians 4:16 "For the Lord himself will come down from heaven, with a loud command, with the voice of the archangel and with the trumpet call of God, and the dead in Christ will rise first."

[2] Before any nation launches a major attack on another, it will evacuate its diplomats and citizens, out of harms way. This would be consistent with a sudden unexplainable disappearance of kingdom citizens and ambassadors from the earth (known as the "rapture" of believers) into the safe zone of a higher dimension, invisible to human eyes, just prior to the kingdom's onslaught.

1 Thessalonians 4:17 "After that, we who are still alive and are left will be caught up together with them in the clouds to meet the Lord in the air. And so we will be with the Lord forever."

Matthew 24:40-41 "Two men will be in the field; one will be taken and the other left. Two women will be grinding with a hand mill; one will be taken and the other left."

Isaiah 57:1 "The righteous perish, and no one ponders it in his heart; devout men are taken away, and no one understands that the righteous are taken away to be spared from evil."

The Bible records an earlier sudden disappearance of a kingdom-minded person, after which, a great flood destroyed the earth. (not unlike kingdom citizens disappearing before the attack on earth)

Appendix 2: Endnotes

Genesis 5:24 "Enoch walked with God; then he was no more, because God took him away."

Hebrews 11:5 "By faith Enoch was taken from this life, so that he did not experience death; he could not be found, because God had taken him away. For before he was taken, he was commended as one who pleased God."

[3] Revelation 21:4 "He will wipe every tear from their eyes. There will be no more death or mourning or crying or pain, for the old order of things has passed away."

1 Corinthians 15:54-55 "When the perishable has been clothed with the imperishable, and the mortal with immortality, then the saying that is written will come true: 'Death has been swallowed up in victory. Where, O death, is your victory? Where, O death, is your sting?'"

[4] John 14:3 "And if I [Jesus] go and prepare a place for you, I will come back and take you to be with me that you also may be where I am."

Not a scriptural reference, but a great musical word picture of all kingdom citizens, entering heaven at the same time: "Oh, when the saints go marching in, Lord how I want to be in that number, when the saints go marching in. Oh, when the trumpet sounds its call, Lord, how I want to be in that number, when the saints go marching in." *Traditional American gospel song, author unknown.*

[5] Revelation 15:2b "standing beside the sea, those who had been victorious over the beast and its image and over the number of its name. They held harps given them by God"

[6] Isaiah 13:4b-5 "The Lord Almighty is mustering an army for war. They come from faraway lands, from the ends of the heavens— the Lord and the weapons of his wrath—to destroy the whole country."

This was a prophecy against Babylon, which, in the Bible, denotes both ancient Persia, as well as the corrupt (present day) 'world order' which God destroys in Revelation 18.

7. Rev 20:4b "And I saw the souls of those who had been beheaded because of their testimony about Jesus and because of the word of God. They had not worshiped the beast or its image and had not received its mark on their foreheads or their hands. They came to life and reigned with Christ a thousand years."

Invasion! Last Call for Citizens
Pages 161 to 168

1. The deal with Lucifer for the earth had a buyback clause. A close relative (of Adam, the human Royal who had lost the earth) has the right to buy back the land. (see note 8, page 207 on the "kinsman redeemer") Jesus bought back the earth with his own blood, but Lucifer was not yielding. Lucifer was in default on the agreement and will later suffer the penalty clauses.

2. The kingdom will release destruction on the earth.

   Revelation 6 tells of the opening of the first four seals on the scroll, which releases the "four horsemen of the Apocalypse," to bring destruction on the earth.

   Revelation 6:1-2 "I watched as the Lamb opened the first of the seven seals. Then I heard one of the four living creatures say in a voice like thunder, "Come!" I looked, and there before me was a white horse! Its rider held a bow, and he was given a crown, and he rode out as a conqueror bent on conquest."

   Two more horses bring war and famine, followed by the fourth ...

   Revelation 6:7-8 "When the Lamb opened the fourth seal, I heard the voice of the fourth living creature say, "Come!" I looked, and there before me was a pale horse! Its rider was named Death, and Hades was following close behind him. They were given power over a fourth of the earth to kill by sword, famine and plague, and by the wild beasts of the earth."

Appendix 2: Endnotes

3   Many from Israel will recognize the Prince and join him.

Revelation 7:4 "Then I heard the number of those who were sealed: 144,000 from all the tribes of Israel."

Revelation 14:1 "Then I looked, and there before me was the Lamb, standing on Mount Zion, and with him 144,000 who had his name and his Father's name written on their foreheads."

The concept of Israel going through great trials and coming to acknowledge the Prince is foreshadowed by the story of Joseph. His brothers, "the sons of Israel," went through many difficulties after trying to kill their brother. Finally, when Joseph revealed himself, they bowed to their brother, who ultimately turned out to be their deliverer. (see note 4, page 218)

4   It is clear to all on earth that the kingdom is behind the attacks.

Revelation 6:15-16 "Then the kings of the earth, the Princes, the generals, the rich, the mighty, and every slave and every free man hid in caves and among the rocks of the mountains. They called to the mountains and the rocks, 'Fall on us and hide us from the face of him who sits on the throne and from the wrath of the Lamb!'"

Revelation 20:4 "And I saw the souls of those who had been beheaded because of their testimony for Jesus and because of the word of God."

5   Revelation 7:16 "Never again will they hunger; never again will they thirst."

6   Stubborn resistance persists, in spite of overwhelming destruction.

Revelation 9:20 "The rest of mankind that were not killed by these plagues still did not repent of the work of their hands; they did not stop worshiping demons, and idols of gold, silver, bronze, stone and wood—idols that cannot see or hear or walk. Nor did they repent of their murders, their magic arts, their sexual immorality or their thefts."

7   Revelation 8:1 "When he opened the seventh seal, there was silence in heaven for about half an hour."

Passport Please - Second Edition

8. The destruction continues—a volcano-induced tsunami?

   Revelation 8:8 "The second angel sounded his trumpet, and something like a huge mountain, all ablaze, was thrown into the sea."

   A collapse of Cumbre Vieja, the most active volcano in the Canary Islands, would generate a dome of water nearly 3,000 ft. high, which would speed across the Atlantic, hitting coastlines from Maine to Brazil with waves over 100 feet high. From *Cumbre Vieja Volcano – Potential Collapse and Tsunami at La Palma, Canary Islands*, (2001) by Steven Ward, University of California Institute of Geophysics and Planetary Physics and Simon Day, University College (UK) Department of Geological Sciences. Information from this paper was widely reprinted by CNN, Popular Mechanics, and many other popular media outlets.

   Nuclear contamination? Revelation 8:10 "The third angel sounded his trumpet, and a great star, blazing like a torch, fell from the sky on a third of the rivers and on the springs of water - the name of the star is Wormwood. A third of the waters turned bitter, and many people died from the waters that had become bitter."

   A web search will quickly reveal much Bible-centered discussion based on the fact that "Chernobyl" is the Ukrainian word for "Wormwood." Chernobyl is a city in Ukraine, the site of the 1986 nuclear disaster, which spread radiation over Russia and Europe.

9. A world leader emerges onto the scene (Darta, in the novel). He is the "beast" described in the Revelation to John.

   Revelation 13:1-10 "It was given authority over every tribe, people, language and nation. All inhabitants of the earth will worship the beast."

   He is followed by a second beast (Runson, in the novel).

   Revelation 13:11-17, who "exercised all the authority of the first beast on its behalf, and made the earth and its inhabitants worship the first beast"

   In Revelation 16:13, that second beast is known as the "false prophet." The two beasts are known as the anti-Christ and the anti-Spirit. With Lucifer (the anti-God), they are the "unholy trinity."

Appendix 2: Endnotes

10   Revelation 13:7 "He [the earthly ruler, the anti-Christ] was given power to make war against the saints and to conquer them."

John 16:2 "a time is coming when anyone who kills you will think they are offering a service to God."

11   Every human will be required to receive the "mark of the beast." Without the mark, buying or selling will be impossible.

Revelation 13:16-18 "It also forced all people, great and small, rich and poor, free and slave, to receive a mark on their right hands or on their foreheads, so that they could not buy or sell unless they had the mark, which is the name of the beast or the number of its name. This calls for wisdom. Let the person who has insight calculate the number of the beast, for it is the number of a man. That number is 666."

12   The new world leader survived an apparently fatal wound.

Rev 13:3-8 "One of the heads of the beast seemed to have had a fatal wound, but the fatal wound had been healed. The whole world was astonished and followed the beast."

13   The first beast (the anti-Christ) will be in power for 3½ years.

Revelation 13:5 "The beast was given a mouth to utter proud words and blasphemies and to exercise its authority for forty-two months."

14   The kingdom army storms the earth.

Revelation 19:14 "The armies of heaven were following him, riding on white horses and dressed in fine linen, white and clean."

Kingdom citizens just arrived from the earth may be part of that horseback army—they had similar uniforms.

Revelation 7:9 "After this I looked, and there before me was a great multitude that no one could count, from every nation, tribe, people and language, standing before the throne and before the Lamb. They were wearing *white robes* and were holding palm branches in their hands."

15. Revelation 19:20 "But the beast was captured and with him the false prophet ... The two of them were thrown alive into the fiery lake of burning sulfur."

16. Revelation 20:1-3 "And I saw an angel coming down out of heaven, having the key to the Abyss and holding in his hand a great chain. He seized the dragon, that ancient serpent, who is the devil, or Satan, and bound him for a thousand years. He threw him into the Abyss, and locked and sealed it over him, to keep him from deceiving the nations anymore until the thousand years were ended."

Revelation 9:2-3a, 10-11 "When he [an angel] opened the Abyss, smoke rose from it like the smoke from a gigantic furnace. The sun and sky were darkened by the smoke from the Abyss. And out of the smoke locusts came down on the earth ... They had tails with stingers, like scorpions, and in their tails they had power to torment people for five months. They had as king over them the angel of the Abyss, whose name in Hebrew is Abaddon and in Greek is Apollyon (that is, Destroyer)."

Luke 8:31 "And they [the demons] begged Jesus repeatedly not to order them to go into the Abyss."

Reestablishing the Garden Colony
Pages 169 to 172

1. Those who committed to the kingdom during the war (the tribulation) and were executed for making that commitment, will be resurrected and will rule the earth with Christ.

Revelation 20:4b, 6 "And I saw the souls of those who had been beheaded because of their testimony for Jesus and because of the word of God. They had not worshiped the beast or his image and had not received his mark on their foreheads or their hands. They came to life and reigned with Christ a thousand years ... Blessed and holy are those who have part in the first resurrection. The second death has no power over them, but they will be priests of God and of Christ and will reign with him for a thousand years."

Appendix 2: Endnotes

During the thousand-year reign of the Prince on earth, Jews will be known for their special relationship with the Prince.

Zechariah 8:3, 7b-8, 23 "I [the Lord] will return to Zion and dwell in Jerusalem... I will save my people from the countries of the east and the west. I will bring them back to live in Jerusalem; they will be my people, and I will be faithful and righteous to them as their God... In those days ten people from all languages and nations will take firm hold of one Jew by the hem of his robe and say, 'Let us go with you, because we have heard that God is with you.'"

2 The Prince rules over a bountiful earth where sickness and death is rare, and long life is common.

Isaiah 65:20-23 "Never again will there be in it an infant who lives but a few days, or an old man who does not live out his years; he who dies at a hundred will be thought a mere youth; he who fails to reach a hundred will be considered accursed. They will build houses and dwell in them; they will plant vineyards and eat their fruit. No longer will they build houses and others live in them, or plant and others eat. For as the days of a tree, so will be the days of my people; my chosen ones will long enjoy the works of their hands. They will not toil in vain or bear children doomed to misfortune; for they will be a people blessed by the Lord, they and their descendants with them."

Last Attack - Crushing Response
Pages 173 to 177

1 Ezekiel 38:2 "Son of man, set your face against Gog, of the land of Magog, the chief Prince of Meshech and Tubal; prophesy against him"

2 Lucifer picks up where he left off.

Revelation 20:7-8 "When the thousand years are over, Satan will be released from his prison and will go out to deceive the nations in the four corners of the earth—Gog and Magog—to gather them for battle. In number they are like the sand on the seashore."

3. Attack on the kingdom!

   Revelation 20:9 "They marched across the breadth of the earth and surrounded the camp of God's people, the city he loves. But fire came down from heaven and devoured them."

4. Revelation 20:10 "And the devil, who deceived them, was thrown into the lake of burning sulfur, where the beast and the false prophet had been thrown. They will be tormented day and night for ever and ever."

5. The heavenly city will be free of evil and corruption.

   Revelation 21:27 "Nothing impure will ever enter it, nor will anyone who does what is shameful or deceitful, but only those whose names are written in the Lamb's book of life."

6: Judgment Day
Trial and Sentencing
Pages 179 to 183

1. Immigration detention is where unauthorized immigrants are held until a decision is made to either allow them into the country, send them back where they came from, or deport them elsewhere.

2. Psalm 50:4 "He summons the heavens above, and the earth, that he may judge his people"

   Daniel 12:2 "Multitudes who sleep in the dust of the earth will awake: some to everlasting life, others to shame and everlasting contempt."

   Joel 3:2 "I will gather all nations and bring them down to the Valley of Jehoshaphat. There I will put them on trial for what they did to my inheritance, my people Israel, because they scattered my people among the nations and divided up my land."

3. Revelation 20:11 "Then I saw a great white throne and him who was seated on it. Earth and sky fled from his presence, and there was no place for them."

Appendix 2: Endnotes

[4] James 5:9b "The Judge is standing at the door!"

[5] Isaiah 3:13 "The Lord takes his place in court; he rises to judge the people."

Acts 17:31 "For he has set a day when he will judge the world with justice by the man he has appointed. He has given proof of this to everyone by raising him from the dead."

[6] John 5:22 "Moreover, the Father judges no one, but has entrusted all judgment to the Son"

[7] Your list of good deeds is not a ticket into the kingdom.

Matthew 7:22-24 "Many will say to me on that day, 'Lord, Lord, did we not prophesy in your name, and in your name drive out demons and perform many miracles?' Then I will tell them plainly, 'I never knew you. Away from me, you evildoers!'"

Romans 3:20a "Therefore, no one will be declared righteous in his sight by observing the law"

[8] The law is not up for debate.

Job 40:6-8 "Then the Lord spoke to Job out of the storm: 'Brace yourself like a man; I will question you, and you shall answer me. Would you discredit my justice? Would you condemn me to justify yourself?'"

[9] God respects anyone's right to reject him.

Luke 12:8-9 "I tell you, whoever acknowledges me before men, the Son of Man will also acknowledge him before the angels of God. But he who disowns me before men will be disowned before the angels of God."

[10] 2 Thessalonians 1:8-9 "He will punish those who do not know God and do not obey the gospel of our Lord Jesus. They will be punished with everlasting destruction and shut out from the presence of the Lord and from the majesty of his power"

11. Leniency is allowed, as long as it is consistent with the law.

    Romans 2:12 "All who sin apart from the law will also perish apart from the law, and all who sin under the law will be judged by the law."

    Romans 4:15 "law brings wrath. And where there is no law there is no transgression."

    Luke 12:48 "But the one who does not know and does things deserving punishment will be beaten with few blows. From everyone who has been given much, much will be demanded; and from the one who has been entrusted with much, much more will be asked."

12. Galatians 6:7 "Do not be deceived: God cannot be mocked. A man reaps what he sows."

13. All the evidence is available to the judge, all secrets revealed.

    Revelation 20:12b "The dead were judged according to what they had done as recorded in the books."

    Matthew 12:37 "For by your words you will be acquitted, and by your words you will be condemned."

    Psalm 90:8 "You have set our iniquities before you, our secret sins in the light of your presence."

    Romans 2:5 "But because of your stubbornness and your unrepentant heart, you are storing up wrath against yourself for the day of God's wrath, when his righteous judgment will be revealed."

14. Revelation 20:15 "If anyone's name was not found written in the book of life, he was thrown into the lake of fire."

    Daniel 12:1 "at that time your people—everyone whose name is found written in the book—will be delivered."

15. Revelation 20:12 "And I saw the dead, great and small, standing before the throne, and books were opened."

Appendix 2: Endnotes

[16] The earth will be cleaned up before it officially becomes part of the kingdom.

Revelation 20:14 "Then death and Hades were thrown into the lake of fire."

2 Peter 3:10-13 "The heavens will disappear with a roar; the elements will be destroyed by fire, and the earth and everything done in it will be burned up.... That day will bring about the destruction of the heavens by fire and the elements will melt in the heat. But in keeping with his promise we are looking forward to a new heaven and a new earth, the home of righteousness."

7: Kingdom Comes to Earth

Immigration Project Debrief
Pages 185 to 187

[1] John 15:13 "Greater love has no one than this, that he lay down his life for his friends."

[2] 1 John 4:19 "We love because he first loved us."

John 3:16 "For God so loved the world that he gave his one and only Son, that whoever believes in him shall not perish but have eternal life."

[3] John 14:16-17 "And I [Jesus] will ask the Father, and he will give you another Counselor to be with you forever— the Spirit of truth. The world cannot accept him, because it neither sees him nor knows him. But you know him, for he lives with you and will be in you."

[4] Revelation 21:3 "And I heard a loud voice from the throne saying, 'Now the dwelling of God is with men, and he will live with them. They will be his people, and God himself will be with them and be their God.'"

The New Adventure
Pages 189 to 190

1. Revelation 21:5b "He who is seated on the throne said, 'I am making everything new!'"

2. Revelation 21:16b, 17 "He measured the city with the rod and found it to be 12,000 stadia in length, and as wide and high as it is long. [about 1400 x 1400 miles] He measured its wall and it was 144 cubits thick [200 feet], by man's measurement, which the angel was using."

3. The whole earth had already been burned up, so the sea that disappeared was likely the "Crystal Sea" in the kingdom.

    2 Peter 3:10 "But the day of the Lord will come like a thief. The heavens will disappear with a roar; the elements will be destroyed by fire, and the earth and everything done in it will be laid bare."

    Revelation 21:1 "Then I saw a new heaven and a new earth, for the first heaven and the first earth had passed away, and there was no longer any sea."

4. Revelation 21:2 "I saw the Holy City, the new Jerusalem, coming down out of heaven from God, prepared as a bride beautifully dressed for her husband."

    Amos 9:6 "he builds his lofty palace in the heavens and sets its foundation on the earth; he calls for the waters of the sea and pours them out over the face of the land—the Lord is his name."

5. It was very noisy the day that New Jerusalem came down.

    Ezra 3:12-13 "But many of the older priests and Levites and family heads, who had seen the former temple, wept aloud when they saw the foundation of this temple being laid, while many others shouted for joy. No one could distinguish the sound of the shouts of joy from the sound of weeping, because the people made so much noise. And the sound was heard far away."

Appendix 2: Endnotes

6   Revelation 21:18-21 "The wall was made of jasper, and the city of pure gold, as pure as glass. The foundations of the city walls were decorated with every kind of precious stone. The first foundation was jasper, the second sapphire, the third chalcedony, the fourth emerald, the fifth sardonyx, the sixth carnelian, the seventh chrysolite, the eighth beryl, the ninth topaz, the tenth chrysoprase, the eleventh jacinth, and the twelfth amethyst. The twelve gates were twelve pearls, each gate made of a single pearl [*the pearly gates*]. The great street of the city was of pure gold, like transparent glass."

7   Jesus prepared this place for his human family.

John 14:3 "And if I [Jesus] go and prepare a place for you, I will come back and take you to be with me that you also may be where I am."

8   *One* tree on *two* sides of the river may imply other dimensions are involved.

Revelation 22:1 "Then the angel showed me the river of the water of life, as clear as crystal, flowing from the throne of God and of the Lamb down the middle of the great street of the city. On *each* side of the river stood *the* tree of life, bearing twelve crops of fruit, yielding its fruit every month."

9   Stick with Jesus and the adventure will continue.

John 1:39 "They said [to Jesus] 'Rabbi, where are you staying?' 'Come,' he replied, 'and you will see.'

Passport Please - Second Edition

KINGDOM OF HEAVEN
DEPARTMENT OF IMMIGRATION

"You have enlarged the nation, Lord;
you have enlarged the nation.
You have gained glory for yourself;
You have extended all the borders of the land."

Isaiah 26:15

For more information on *Passport Please*, discussion groups, the Discussion Guide, and the upcoming movie adaptation of *Passport Please*, visit:

www.passport-please.com